Donated by
Joseph and Diane Bast
to The Heartland Institute
2015

C0-DKP-218

SHE SHOULD HAVE BEEN
President

THE WISDOM OF DIXY LEE RAY

WITH LOU GUZZO

Outkirts Press, Inc.
Denver, Colorado

The opinions expressed in this manuscript are solely the opinions of the author and do not represent the opinions or thoughts of the publisher. The author represents and warrants that s/he either owns or has the legal right to publish all material in this book.

She Should Have Been President
The Wisdom of Dixy Lee Ray
All Rights Reserved
Copyright © 2007 With Lou Guzzo

Cover Image © 2007 JupiterImages Corporation
All Rights Reserved. Used With Permission.

This book may not be reproduced, transmitted, or stored in whole or in part by any means, including graphic, electronic, or mechanical without the express written consent of the publisher except in the case of brief quotations embodied in critical articles and reviews.

Outskirts Press
http://www.outskirtspress.com

ISBN-10: 1-59800-875-7
ISBN-13: 978-1-59800-875-3

Outskirts Press and the "OP" logo are trademarks belonging to
Outskirts Press, Inc.

Printed in the United States of America

DEDICATED TO THE
SUSAN G. KOMEN
BREAST CANCER FOUNDATION AND TO
ALL THE GALLANT SOULS WHO WORK
FOR IT AND SUPPORT ITS GOALS

PREFACE

Dixy Lee Ray was one of a kind --- an internationally renowned marine scientist and an enormously gifted, intelligent human being with an incredible memory and an IQ in the clouds. At various times in her life, she was also lovable and caring, remarkably generous, and ingenious on one hand and impatient with trivia, intolerant with the ignorant, and fiercely private on the other.

For all those reasons and, most important, because she knew how to solve many of the nation's most serious economic and energy problems, she should have been President of the United States of America. She came very close to consideration for that exalted position. President Gerald Ford wanted her as his White House science adviser; then President Ronald Reagan, also a good friend, wanted her as his cabinet science chief, a job for which she was admirably suited and qualified. But, as she learned later, the politicos in Ford's and Reagan's camps had vetoed her selection because she "would have been too feisty" and would have antagonized the anti-nuclear and environmental protesters.

This book is well timed. It is published as several women are being considered for the lofty position of President of the United States. Not one of them could come close to Dixy Lee Ray in intelligence, experience, and imagination. However, if one of them should be elected as America's first woman President, she could find great wisdom, ideas, and inspiration in this book.

The chapters in this book will demonstrate conclusively that she had the wisdom and imagination that would have been great for America in these explosive times. She had already had a taste for democracy, its foibles, and its remarkable benefits. Service as chairman of the old U.S. Atomic Energy Commission, as an assistant secretary of state and director of the new Bureau of Oceans and International Environmental and Scientific Affairs, and, finally, as the first woman Governor of Washington State gave her more than enough experience to run a country.

In addition, Dr. Ray had traveled extensively to serve as a consultant on marine-science and oceanographic matters in the Middle East, Italy, the Scandinavian countries, Singapore, Australia, China, and Malaysia. She had also served as chief officer of a seagoing investigation of sea life in the Pacific and Indian Oceans aboard a vessel owned and operated by Stanford University, a school at which she had won her doctorate in marine science. She also was the U.S. representative to the crucial Law of the Seas organization, which included every nation bordering ocean shores in the world.

Dr. Ray would have made a great President, not only because of her brilliance as a scientist and an administrator, but also because criticism from the news media or any other quarter never caused her to deviate from a decision based on principle. Maybe she would have lasted only one term as President, but what a dynamic term it would have been! These chapters clearly indicate what vision and brilliance she would have brought to the major problems of the nation.

One of the strongest examples of the reasons she would have made an outstanding President was her 1973 report to President Nixon on solving the energy crisis for all time. As the A.E.C. chairman, she gathered together the brightest scientific minds in the nation from public and private life and fashioned an extraordinary report titled "The Nation's Energy Future." When she presented the finished product to Nixon, he was already stung by the Watergate scandal and consigned the report to a shelf in his office. If implemented, the report would have solved America's energy problems for all time and there would have been no need to become involved in the affairs of the oil-rich Middle East --- or any other oil-producing country.

If her report had been approved by Congress --- and there was an excellent chance of that happening in the tumultuous period that O.P.E.C. had orchestrated the oil shortage in 1973--- we would have had no need to become reliant on foreign oil. The details are in Chapter 11. What Nixon failed to do, Dr. Ray could have done easily as America's first woman President.

Her life could be divided into two very distinct parts. Through most of it, and particularly in her early teaching days, she was much loved and admired, not only by her students but by the public and, specially, by members of the news media. At the University of Washington, where she taught biology and marine science for three decades, she was voted one of the most popular teachers on more than one occasion in campus-wide polls.

The second part of her life began when she left academia for public service, first as chairman of the powerful Atomic Energy Commission and then as an assistant secretary of state under Henry Kissinger. Now, regarded as a "political" appointee and a Conservative, she fell out of favor with the Liberals in the news media and could never understand why. Neither could I, who worked with her at the A.E.C., the State Department, and the Washington State Governor's office, where I served as her chief policy adviser.

The media antagonism intensified and became vitriolic when she returned home from Washington, D.C. to run for the governorship and won election. Neither she nor I could understand how a woman who was for many years the "darling of the press" suddenly became the "enemy of the press."

I think I understand it now, years after her death in January, 1994. Dixy's impatience with trivia and ignorance translated itself into impatience with the frequently ridiculous questions and unfounded suspicions of many reporters and editors in both the print and broadcast media. It was not unusual for her to glare at a reporter and say, "Now, that's a silly question. You want to try again?" Wouldn't it be refreshing to hear a President say that to the errant press these days!

Because of her lifelong devotion to scientific truth and that impatience with trivia, she made enemies fast in the news media. The fact was that, despite her brilliance and imaginative outlook on all issues, she was not suited to the political life --- but she should have been a refreshing newcomer to that topsy-turvy land. When I tried to tell her she should be patient with the press, she would shake her head defiantly and say, "They will accept me for what I am or lump it!" Defiant to the last.

She was defeated in her bid for re-election, thanks to a major defection in her own Democratic Party. But it may have been just as well. When she had first decided to enter politics, she and all the rest of her friends knew she was better suited to the Republican Party's Conservative principles, but when her predecessor, Republican Dan Evans, delayed making a decision about running for an unprecedented fourth term, she was told she had to make up her mind because she needed to start fund-raising activities.

At the time, she told me: "Oh, nuts! I can't wait for Dan to make up his mind. My father was a Democrat, so I may as well run as a Democrat." No Democrat in American history has been more Conservative than Dixy Lee Ray!

In her four years as Governor, Dixy worked hard to cut the state budget, the size of state government, and unnecessary spending, actions that angered the Liberal Democrats but pleased the few Democratic Conservatives in the Legislature and, of course, all the Republicans.

Despite her hectic years in the political arena nationally and at home, I still resent the fact that Dixy failed to receive the acclaim she richly deserved in her earlier years. It was Dr. Dixy Lee Ray, the scientist and teacher, who was most responsible for the creation of the marvelous University of Washington scientific research station at Friday Harbor. It was also Dr. Ray, one of the Pacific Northwest's pioneer environmentalists, whose report to the State Legislature helped save the Nisqually River Valley from incursions by industry.

It was also Dr. Ray, whose one-woman campaign helped save the whales of the North Pacific and Puget Sound from extinction at the hands of foreign and American whalers. And it was also Dr. Ray, whose energy and imagination helped create the Pacific Science Center, which remains one of the jewels of the Seattle Center.

In all these endeavors and many more, she had the support and influence of one of the most powerful men in national politics, Washington State's Senator Warren G. Magnuson. And yet, it was the senator, who, like the news-media enviros, turned against Dr. Ray, because she wanted the Coast Guard to protect and patrol Puget Sound from all polluters, instead of banning virtually all transports from the Sound, a ridiculous and unnecessary --- and terribly expensive --- action.

As a daily columnist and, later, as managing editor of the Seattle Post-Intelligencer, I worked with Dixy on numerous environmental issues. Then along came Rachel Carlson's scientifically flawed book, "Silent Spring," and the environmental movement was taken over by the loud-mouthed extremists. That's when Dixy and I left the environmental movement we had pioneered in the Northwest and eventually wrote the two protest books, _Trashing the Planet_ and _Environmental Overkill_, which were appeals for a sane, balanced, and scientifically accurate approach to environmental issues. A sensible, scientifically based environmental policy was one of many programs she could have pursued as President.

Both books were successful and sold more than a quarter-million copies each. We had at least three more books researched and ready for the writing when Dixy died of a severe respiratory ailment in January, 1994. Sadly, I put all our research and the articles and chapters we had amassed on the shelf. Recently, a good friend persuaded me to finish the job and select the best pieces for at least one more book in her name and mine. This is it.

The chapters in this book are a tribute to Dixy's extraordinary mind, her imaginative spirit, and her vision of the future. I had a hand in many of the chapters, but they are, for the most part, the work of one of the most creative and misunderstood women of all time, Dixy Lee Ray, who should have been President.

---LG

TABLE OF CONTENTS

Chapter 1 --- Promise Them Anything --- How governments grow and politicians and the number of workers grow with them.

Chapter 2 --- The Wheeler Dealers --- A true-life account of how the new Governor countered efforts of two scheming Democratic politicos to involve her in dishonest deals.

Chapter 3 --- The Greatest Worry --- A history of war and the logic behind America's use of nuclear bombs to end the Second World War; who better to explain it than the former chief of the U.S. Atomic Energy Commission?

Chapter 4 --- Nuclear Arms Control and Test Bans --- Why we should continue the U.S. testing program.

Chapter 5 --- The Theory of a "Just War" --- Why and when war is justified and necessary.

Chapter 6 --- Time for a New Environmental Policy --- Why U.S. must have a sensible approach to environmental issues.

Chapter 7 --- Environmental Law --- The laws and regulations propounded by the Liberals concerning environmental issues are out of control.

Chapter 8 --- Another Outrageous E.P.A. Ban --- The ridiculous action the Liberals invoked against methyl bromide, the farmers' friend.

Chapter 9 --- Overdue: A Supreme Court of Science --- One of Dr. Ray's favorite topics.

Chapter 10 --- The Mouse Is Still Roaring --- The nations we have fed are biting the hand that feeds them.

Chapter 11 --- A Permanent End to the Energy Crisis --- The ingenious plan Dr. Ray presented to President Nixon but which never saw the light of day.

Chapter 12 --- News Media Shakeup Due --- All the media should quit accepting the wild environmental charges the Ultraliberal enviros make as gospel.

Chapter 13 --- The Greatest Threat to America --- The nation's worst enemies are big government and the welfare state, both promoted by Democratic Party Liberals.

Chapter 14 ---Two-Party System Falling Apart --- The Democratic Party's plunge toward Socialism has upset the important, historic political balance.

Chapter 15 --- The Teacher Speaks Her Mind --- Dr. Ray's brilliant advice to educators.

Chapter 16--- About That Dirty Word: Waste --- Some sensible advice about waste management from a real expert.

Chapter 17 --- Rediscovering Living Plants --- The scientific case for more plants and trees.

Chapter 18 --- Energy for the World --- On the importance of energy to all nations.

Chapter 19 --- Short Takes --- The author's opinions on a variety of topics.

Chapter 20 --- Prologue: A New Approach --- An urgent appeal for common sense.

CHAPTER 1
PROMISE *THEM ANYTHING*

*O*riginally, this statement by Dr. Ray was written as a prologue to her autobiography, which she and I were beginning to assemble at the time of her death. In fact, "Promise Them Anything" was a title preferred by both of us for the autobiography. This onetime prologue represents Dixy's greatest fear for America --- the catastrophe that could be ahead as national, state, and local governments continued to seize power and lead to the establishment of socialism. At one time, we had considered the title "Goodbye, America," but were persuaded to switch to "Environmental Overkill," which we eventually titled our second book. Here, then, like a somber voice from the grave, is the beginning chapter of her warning to the land she loved so much.

***

The central question in the United States today is whether we can, in fact, govern ourselves. Of course, there are many issues of great importance to our survival as a nation: How to assure an adequate and dependable supply of energy at reasonable cost, the intelligent use of natural resources, achieving a proper balance between compassion and self-reliance in social problems, credible military strength, and demonstrable economic health.

But all of these depend, for national policies to be successful, upon a knowledgeable majority of supportive citizerns. And herein lies our present dilemma. Few know what really goes on in government, and those who do know seldom talk about it ... honestly. Those who do understand what's happening to self-government and write about it accurately are not widely read.

In their percipient book, <u>The Political Economy of Federal Government Growth</u>, Bennett and Johnson, commenting on the size and intrusiveness of the federal agovernment, noted correctly that "... the reason government has grown is that those individuals who benefit most from government growth, bureaucrats and politicians, have been able to increase the size and scope of government because voters have been led to believe that the benefits from government involvement in 'crises' far exceed any reasonable estimate of associated costs."

Politicians and bureaucrats work at survival through promising virtually anything, whether it is impractical, impossible, or dishonest. Big government has become self-perpetuating and costly beyond reckoning. Among the reasons for this is the willingness of too many intelligent, capable citizens to leave the business of government up to politicians, career people who make the art of holding public office a lifetime pursuit.

For self-government to succeed, there cannot be a class of politicians, but that's what we have, and breaking into their ranks is a chancy and uncommon thing. Added to this is a growing horde of public servants, bureaucrats, regulators, and staff, not answerable to the voters but constituting a shadow government with real power, increasingly centralized. And none of them elected by the people!

What should we do? For starters, we should diligently pursue the steps we must take to reduce the size and scope of government and return more authority and responsibility to local and state governments --- for only when the governmental unit is small enough and near enough can citizens hope to know what it is doing.

In A New Message, Jackson Pemberton put it this way: "In order to thwart the designs of self-seeking men, we set up three branches of government, each equal in power but separate in authority and function, and each with certain limited but effective sanctions upon the two others. We reserved most of the powers of government to the states, thus dividing those powers and placing them as close as possible to the inspection and control of the people, for history has abundantly shown that centralization of power and tyranny are but different titles for the same monster."

It may be that relating one person's experiences in high government posts, both at the national and state levels, will help illuminate some of the reasons our government has become tyrannical. It may be that knowing what it's like will encourage some to "go into politics" who would otherwise have stayed away from "that dirty business." I hope so, because...

"A democracy cannot survive as a permanent form of government. It can only survive until the voters discover that they can vote themselves largesse from the public treasury. From that time on, the majority of citizens will vote for the candidate promising the greatest benefits from the public purse, with the result that a democracy always collapses from loose fiscal policies, always followed by a dictatorship.

"The average age (survival time) of the world's greatest democratic nations and societies has been 200 years! Each has gone through the same sequence:

"From bondage to spirtual faith.
"From spiritual faith to great courage.
"From courage to liberty.
"From liberty to abundance.
"From abundance to complacency.
"From complacency to selfishness.
"From selfishness to apathy.
"From apathy to dependency, and
"From dependency back into bondage...

"Fortunately, the record shows that people can regain their faith, understanding, and courage. They can again become persons and citizens who are responsible for their own welfare, rather than units and subjects identified by numbers for purposes of regimentation and subsidization. The record shows that people can, by their own intelligent actions, regain their liberty any time they want it."

I have adapted and paraphrased these quotations from a variety of sources, including Alexander Frazer Tyler, Lord Thomas B. Macaulay, and Dean Russell's <u>A Short History of Liberty</u>, which appeared in <u>The Freeman</u> in January, 1955. And I have used them freely and often in speeches and articles, because they superbly illustrate my point. It doesn't matter that the quotations are sometimes attributed to others.

Everything depends, then, upon knowing what is really going on in government so as to be free from those who promise them anything.

CHAPTER 2
THE WHEELER DEALERS

*D*ixy Lee Ray, Washington State's first woman governor, had already learned some important basics in politics with her grasp of the "promise them anything" stance. But her bitterest lesson in politics came very early in her first year as Governor. This chapter was also to be included in the autobiography that never was finished. Suffice it to say that it added considerable wisdom to an already wise scientist-turned-public servant.

***

"Tell me, Governor. What do you really want?"

The question, coming after an hour or two of inconsequential talk, struck me like a lightning bolt. It was softly spoken, almost murmured by the Senate Majority Leader, Gordon Walgren, as he leaned forward in his chair, the movement as gentle as his voice. He was watching me intently, his face impassive as he sipped his drink. My mind erupted with alarm bells, but I responded as calmly as I could.

"What do I want? I want to do the best job I can. I want to be remembered as a good governor. I think that the people of this state deserve better than they've been getting. Just good government. That's what I want."

It fell pretty flat. Senator Walgren just sat there looking at me, incredulous, and John Bagnariol, Speaker of the House of Representatives, growled:

"Whattaya mean, good government?"

I looked through the window of the tiny, one-room, A-frame cabin on the shore of Puget Sound. Across the bay the deep green foliage of Douglas Firs reached nearly to the beach, and the sun, low on the horizon, painted the water's surface in colors from gold to mellow red. Peaceful and beautiful, I thought. How strangely it contrasted with the tension and suspicion in that room.

Walgren faced me across the table, set for this occasion in the middle of the room and now strewn with the remains of the evening meal. Bagnariol was to my right, at the table's end, regarding me as one might look at a specimen, somewhat distastefully, with hooded eyes. I felt trapped and uncomfortable. A small fire burned at my back, and there were two security men within sight but out of earshot on the beach outside.

These two men, leaders of the Legislature and the most powerful figures in the state's Democratic Party, seemed to fill the small room with their overbearing presence, silently waiting for me to explain myself.

How could I tell them I was only beginning, with reluctance, to look behind the political façade in Olympia and that I didn't like what I saw? They'd been in the Legislature many years. They knew how it worked. They'd come up through the ranks and were part of the system and key to its power structure. How could I tell them of the many ordinary citizens I had met while campaigning who had held my hand and told me with great feeling but without sentiment or passion, "I don't know you, but I'm going to vote for you because I think you'll make government honest"?

How could I tell them of the reaction I got from Harold Shefelman, distinguished lawyer, respected elder statesman in Seattle, and confidant of several Governors, when I proposed to run for the state's highest office? He fell back against his tall desk chair and, in a shocked voice, said, "Dixy, why would you let yourself in for all that filthy, morally corrupt, mean, and dirty stuff?"

At the time, I didn't appreciate what he had said, but I was beginning to.

How could I tell these two men of the love and pride I had for our state and our nation? I'd been in the federal government and I'd seen plenty of meanness and backbiting and selfish ambition, but I'd seen idealism, too, and honor and personal sacrifice. Could I tell them how much these things meant to me? I tried, but it fell on unbelieving ears.

The three of us were having a private meeting, our first --- and last, to be sure. I had been inaugurated on January 12, 1977, and it was now late May, four months into a stormy Legislative session. Mine was a surprise victory, won over experienced and ambitious politicians, with indifferent support from the Democratic Party.

Some Democrats, mostly moderate to conservative in political philosophy, did support me and worked hard for my election. But my victory resulted from the votes of independents and not a few moderate Republicans. Washington is not a strong "party state." An open primary and independent voting are long established traditions. From the Democratic Party's vocal left wing, I had only grudging support or outright opposition. And from the oldtime Democratic politicians and party leaders in elective office, I was regarded, for the most part, with ill-disguised suspicion.

From the start, I was uneasy about the meeting. Why had Walgren asked for it? I met weekly with the legislative leadership, the Democrats at breakfast, and the Republicans at lunch. My door was open, the phone available. I returned calls from legislataors and tried at all times to be open and receptive, but in those early days few came in or called.

I can never forget the Friday afternoon of a particularly contentious week that saw members of the Olympia press corps trying to outdo each other in the number of scathing remarks and antagonistic statements they could elicit from members of the political opposition. It was still early in the legislative session when my office door swung open and Senator August Mardesich, former majority leader, strode in with half a dozen senators in tow.

"Boss," he said, "I like what you're saying and trying to do, and from now on, we're going to help you."

It was true. From that moment on, I could count on him. Augie's word was always good. Significantly, Walgren, although he was the majority leader, was not one of the group that day. Indeed, during the nearly six months of the 1977 session, I saw little of Senator Walgren. It was a surprise, therefore, when he came to my office alone, proposing a private dinner to include only himself, Bagnariol, and me. He suggested we go "somewhere where we won't be observed."

"It was time," the Senator said, "for the three of us to talk, to get better acquainted, to discuss some things seriously."

I readily agreed, although I thought to myself, "Why be secretive about it?" Surely the Democratic leadership in the Legislature (Democrats were the majority in both House and Senate in 1977) could meet with the Democratic Governor without raising eyebrows!

I was to learn later that little happens "out front" in the Legislature. Most decisions are made, actions taken, and agreements struck in private sessions, whose details never see the light of day. By the time a bill reaches the floor, it's mostly <u>pro forma</u>. So much for "open government."

Anyhow, I thought, if Walgren and Bagnariol want to meet privately with me, good. Maybe I'm making some progress; no questions asked. By all means, let's go! We agreed to use a small private beach cabin not far from Olympia, a place I'd been offered for "getting away from it all." I suggested it as a location more private than any restaurant, and I proposed to send out food from the Executive Mansion.

We'd been at the cabin since early evening, had eaten a good dinner of fried chicken, tossed salad, and rolls, and, now, with a small fire dissipating the coolness that came with sundown, we shifted back to whiskey from the dinner wine.

It was about 9 o'clock when Walgren's question came. Up

until them, not one word had been uttered on pending legislation, basic education (the prime issue of the 1977 session), budget outlays, reorganization of the executive branch, or any other matter that ought to interest the elected heads of state government.

I was determined not to ask what the purpose of the strange little meeting was, nor to take any initiative in directing the conversation, so it continued desultorily until Walgren's bombshell question came, without warning …. "What do you really want?"

He blinked when I replied, "Just good government…," and, like Bagnariol, asked what I meant by that.

"Well, it's time to bring a lot of things under control," I said, lamely. "Like favoritism in purchasing, giving contracts to friends without competitive bidding (as required by state law), the selling of legislation and bank charters, and influence-peddling in general."

I didn't realize it at the time, but I must have struck a very sensitive nerve with my innocent statement about selling legislation and peddling influence!

The blank looks on their faces told me I wasn't making any points --- or friends --- in that room that night. Bagnariol sneered as he asked how I proposed to bring all this about.

"Maybe I'll start with the liquor board case," I said, thinking I'd get a reaction about a hushed up charge of wrongdoing that could possibly embarrass the preceding Republican administration. No response.

The talk petered out around 10 o'clock. I stood up, and the State Patrol security officers who had been keeping the cabin under observation all evening saw me through the window and came to the door, asking if we were ready to return to Olympia. Walgren and Bagnariol were only too happy to terminate the curiously unproductive meeting, so we packed up and climbed the path to where my car was parked.

Sitting in silence between them on the way home, I remember my thoughts. Whatever this test was, I reflected, I certainly flunked it! Could it be that these two men, the political powers in the state, really thought I had to have some ulterior motive for becoming Governor, that I wanted something other than to govern honorably and honestly, and that, having entered politics, my motivation had to be self-serving --- and even illegal?

Could it be that these two men, who actually ran the Legislature, had some motive other than serving the citizens of the state? Obviously, they did. Three years later, they stood in Federal Court, convicted on charges of racketeering. They had been accused of an attempt to sell the state to organized crime and open it up to professional gambling for an 18 percent share of the profits!

Who was Senator Walgren? At first, I didn't take the Senate Majority Leader seriously. I thought of him as a weakling, a figurehead majority leader, content to hold the appearance of leadership without any of the substance. I thought he was willing to live in the shadow of the Senate's real leader, August Mardesich. It was to Mardesich that most legislators, Democrats and Republicans alike, turned to for advice and guidance on the flow of bills.

But I was wrong about Walgren. After Mardesich's defeat in his race to win re-election to the Senate in November, 1978, Walgren emerged as a force to be reckoned with. His treatment of the Republican minority in organizing the 1979 Senate undoubtedly led to the fall of such efficient Republican stalwarts as Senators Jim Matson and Charles Newschwander and the successful coup by the far-right Republican wing, led by Senator Jeanette Rayner. The upper body of the Legislature was crippled by these developments, which helped more Republicans and the Senate itself, eventually, toward an almost reactionary conservatism. It was not my kind of conservatism.

Walgren solidified his leadership position throughout 1979 and early 1980. This pudgy figure, with his bland, impassive face, belied a character of cunning and ruthless self-interest.

And who was John Bagnariol? Unlike Walgren, whose early impression on me was bleak, the Speaker of the House left an indelible imprint. I'll never forget the first time I met him. It was one of those strange political gatherings in a private home meant to introduce a potential candidate to the party faithful.

The time was late summer, 1975. My name had surfaced as a possible gubernatorial candidate, and a close friend on the University of Washington faculty had arranged a Sunday afternoon reception at his Seattle home. Among the dozen or so who attended were Mike Ryherd, former King County Democratic chairman; Karen Marchioro, the reigning county Democratic chairman, who was also the spokesman for the Far Left liberal wing of the party, and Bagnariol.

I'd heard of Baggy, as most persons called him, and was curious to meet the man being heralded as the coming leader of the state's Democratic Party. We faced each other in the living room.

"So you think you want to run for Governor?" he asked in his gravelly voice.

I looked at him directly and saw his eyes go blank, hooded by enormous dark brows. Watch out for this guy, said my mind, unbidden. He wants to be Governor and will do anything to get there. I answered noncommittally that I was merely testing the water, but we were sizing each other up. Clearly he didn't like what he saw, and neither did I.

Bagnariol looked like the small-time, wheeler-dealing, boondoggling, backroom politician, up from the streets, that he was. One of his early business associates described him as likeable and good company in a locker room but "phony as a $9 bill." What an accurate characterization that turned out to be!

We were destined to see a lot of each other, and on occasion to have to work together. Only rarely did our mutual animosity flair into public view, but it was well known to the press. Bagnariol saw to that, and the political reporters in Olympia lapped it up like spaghetti.

"Tell me where the Governor is on this question," Bagnariol used to say to lobbyists and others seeking help on issues or legislation. "If she's for it, I'm against it. If she's against it, then I'll work my tail off for it."

My unexpected election to the office of Governor in 1977 upset a lot of apple carts. The King County Democrats (that's Seattle) were unhappy because I was not one of them, and they sensed I was unsympathetic to their ultraliberal causes. The Republicans were outraged. They had held the governorship for 12 years and benefited from favored treatment in the conduct of state business. I had derailed their plan for succession.

Several prominent Democrats with gubernatorial ambitions were annoyed because I upset their timetables --- Bagnariol for one, but also Representative (and later Senator) A. N. "Bud" Shinpoch, who was building his reputation as a legislative leader by opposing and harassing the Executive.

Walgren also toyed with the idea from time to time, but he vacillated and flirted alternately with the notions of being Governor, attorney general, or remaining a senator --- and finally, perhaps most importantly, revealed that what he really wanted most was power.

The political press, especially in Olympia and Seattle, was furious at my election and tried in my first month to promote a recall movement. I was not, and never would be, "their" Governor.

In the meantime, at that reception at my friend's home, I left Bagnariol in the living room and drifted toward the kitchen, where voices indicated a lively debate was under way. My entry stopped all talk. Quite a welcome, I thought! Mrs. Marchioro, the county Demo boss, whirled and said, almost shouting in my face:

"You have no right to run for Governor!"

"Why not?" I asked, my dander up.

"Because you haven't earned it. You haven't worked in the party. You haven't labored in the fields. You're not qualified."

I have never backed down from a fight, and I certainly wasn't about to start now with this pipsqueak of a professional politician.

Staring her down, I said in a firm, angry voice, "The last time I looked, the qualifications included citizenship and a minimum age. I don't recall party work as being a qualifying requirement for candidacy."

So ended our first encounter.

One can easily understand why my term was filled with so many internal party squabbles and backbiting. But, worst of all, the liberal members of the press were a great disappointment. Wined and dined and kowtowed to by the likes of Bagnariol and Walgren, the reporters swallowed their diatribe and came to view me as a villain. Little wonder that I lost their support and their friendship when I dared take the helm in the state capital.

I wondered if the governors of the 49 other states had to go through the same bitter experiences I endured. Or did some of them capitulate and play the game of enriching themselves at the expense of good government and the state's citizens?

CHAPTER 3
THE GREATEST WORRY: NUCLEAR WAR

Without question, the concern over the possibility of a nuclear war is the dominating issue in the world today. Who is better qualified to comment on the awesome subject than the former chairman of the U.S. Atomic Energy Commission, Dr. Dixy Lee Ray?

***

More than half a century has gone by since the first --- and only --- use of nuclear weapons. The prevailing attitude about the possibility of their future use appears to be a widespread fear amounting to dread.

Despite all those years of non-use and the millions of war deaths from conventional weapons, nuclear strategy still dominates all military and political discussions and all arms-control talks.

A second attitude pervades the community of anti-war, usually Leftist intellectual thinkers. It's the notion that A-bombs, as they were called at the beginning of the Nuclear Age, ought never to have been used at all.

As a prelude to consideration of the vexing problems of nuclear weapons and nuclear war in today's world, it is useful and instructive to recall the circumstances and the reasons for the only atomic bombs ever detonated in war, those dropped on Hiroshima and Nagasaki in 1945.

In historical perspective, the story really began in the year 1281 A.D., when two magnificent Chinese fleets set sail for the empire of Japan. Their purpose was to launch a massive invasion of the Japanese home islands and to conquer Japan in the name of the great Mongol warrior, Kublai Khan. Sailing from China was the main armada, consisting of 3,500 ships and more than 100,000 heavily armed troops. Sailing from ports in Korea was a second impressive fleet of 900 ships with an additional 42,000 Mongolian warriors.

In the summer of that year, the invasion force sailing from Korea arrived off the Western shores of the southernmost island of Japan, Kyushu. The Mongols maneuvered their ships into position and methodically launched their assault upon the coast. Like a human surf, wave after wave of the Oriental soldiers swept the shore at Hagata Bay, where they were met on the beaches by thousands of Japanese defenders, who had never had their homeland invaded successfully.

The Mongol invasion force was a modern army --- modern for the time, that is. Its arsenal of weapons was far superior to anything the Japanese had. Its soldiers were equipped with poison arrows, maces, iron swords, metal javelins, and even gun powder. The Japanese were forced to defend themselves with bows and arrows, swords, spears made from bamboo, and shields made of wood.

The battle was fierce, and many soldiers were killed or wounded on both sides. It raged on for days, but, aided by the fortifications along their beaches, of which the Mongols had had no previous knowledge, and inspired by the sacred cause of defending their homeland, the ancient Japanese warriors pushed the much stronger Mongol forces back to their ships lying at anchor in the bay.

The Mongol fleet then went back out to sea, where it rendezvoused with the second invasion fleet, which was just then arriving from China. In the summer of 1281, the combined forces of foreign invaders maneuvered offshore in preparation for the second assault upon the western shores of Kyushu.

Everywhere in Japan elaborate Shinto ceremonies were performed at shrines in cities and in the countryside. Hundreds of thousands of Japanese, urged on by their emperor and their warlords and other officials, prayed to their Shinto gods for deliverance from these foreign invaders, who had come to defile their homeland. A million Japanese voices called for divine intervention.

Miraculously, almost as if it were an answer to their prayers, a savage typhoon sprang from out of the south and headed toward Kyushu. Its powerful wind screamed up the coast, where it struck the Mongol invasion ships with full fury, wreaking havoc upon them and the men on board. The Mongol fleet was devastated.

After the typhoon had run its course, more than 4,000 invasion craft had been lost and Mongol casualties amounted to more than 100,000. Throughout Japan ceremonies of celebration were held, and the people thanked their Shinto gods for the divine wind that had come to remove the invading force.

Six hundred sixty four years passed. It was the summer of 1945. The Second World War had been raging in the Pacific, and now another invasion force composed of Americans, with some Australian allies, was poised to invade Japan.

Very few people knew then and even fewer know now about the details of the American plan for invasion of the Japanese homeland It was code-named "Operation Downfall." Like the Mongols before them, the foreign invaders would arrive in two powerful invasion fleets. One, departing from Okinawa and code-named "Operation Olympic," would set sail in October, 1945, and arrive off Kyushu on November 1. Depending upon the results of that invasion, a second force would be launched against the main island of Honshu with the goal of occupying the Tokyo Plain by March 1, 1946.

The initial invading force consisted of more than 550,000

American soldiers, accompanied by tens of thousands of Marines, sailors, and aviators. There were 4,000 aircraft poised at Okinawa alone. The overwhelming invasion force would consist of thousands of ships, from aircraft carriers to landing craft. They would sail from Okinawa, the Philippines, and the Marianas.

Such a fleet could not be gathered secretly, and the Japanese knew of its coming and, therefore, made preparations. Throughout the summer of 1945, the emperor and his government officials exhorted the military and the civilian population to make preparations for the coming invasion. Again, as in 1281, fortifications were built. This time they were mainly underground --- and they were not known to the American invading force.

Thousands of suicide aircraft were constructed by the Japanese. They were planes with just enough power and just enough gas to make one flight and then to crash down upon the invaders. Underground factories were built in all regions of Japan, and in those factories, suicide boats and suicide submarines were constructed. Again, they had just enough power and fuel to carry the boat or sub to the target and then crash.

Armies were moved to the south to protect the shores of Kyushu, since the Japanese authorities surmised correctly that it would be the area attacked first. Schools were closed and children were given materials and instruction on how to use weapons and how to make hand grenades.

Everywhere in the countryside, civilian attack units were formed. All through the summer, Japanese radio cried out to the people to form a wall of human flesh and push the American invaders back into their ships and into the sea. They fervently believed that their homeland could never be invaded successfully.

But something happened on the way to the invasion. On August 6, the first atomic bomb was dropped on Hiroshima and on August 9, the second bomb fell on Nagasaki. On August 14, the unconditional surrender was signed. The war in the Pacific was over and the Second World War came to an abrupt end.

Almost immediately, the invasion-force personnel prepared to be evacuated out of Okinawa, the Philippines, and other Pacific islands for a return to the U.S. The operation, code-named "Magic Carpet," was undertaken right away, but just as it had taken weeks to assemble the invasion forces, it also took considerable time to ship them home.

By October 1, there were only about 200,000 troops lelft on Okinawa, and they were still evacuating personnel. Buckner Bay, on the East Coast of Okinawa, was still jammed with vessels of all kinds, from victory ships to landing craft. There were 150,000 soldiers living in "tent cities," rows and rows of tents thoughout the island. Hundreds of tons of food and equipment and surplus supplies of all kinds, which had been gathered for the invasion, were still stacked out in the open on Okinawa.

Now, it happened that during the early part of October, to the southwest of Okinawa and just northeast of the Marianas, the seas began to grow restless, the sky grew dark, and the winds began to blow. The ocean turned dark and the large swells that were developing began to churn the surface with foam.

In a matter of only a few days, in the first week of October, a gigantic typhoon had somehow, out of season, sprung up, come to life, and begun to sweep past Saipan and in the Philippine Sea. As the storm grew more violent, it raced northward and kicked up waves that were 60 feet high.

Navy meteorologists eventually became aware of the storm (there were no weather satellites, of course, and no Nimbus pictures at the time). But the meteorologists expected the storm to pass between Formosa and Okinawa and disappear into the East China Sea. Unexplainably, on the evening of October 8, the storm changed directions abruptly and headed toward the east.

When it did so, there was no time to get up steam and there was insufficient warning to allow the ships that were in the harbors at Okinawa to move out to sea and escape the typhoon's terrible violence. By late morning on the 9th of October, rain was coming down in torrents, the seas were rising, and visibility was zero.

Winds were now blowing at more than 80 miles an hour, causing the small craft to drag their anchors. By early afternoon, the wind had risen over the 100-mile-an-hour mark and rain came in horizontally, its waters both fresh and salty. And even larger vessels began dragging their anchors in the pounding of the 50-foot seas.

As the winds continued to increase and the storm unleashed its maximum power, the entire Buckner Bay became a sea of devastation. Ships dragged their anchors, colliding with other ships; hundreds of vessels were blown ashore; vessels in groups of two or three crashed into each other or were washed ashore into the piles of wreckage on the beaches.

By mid-afternoon, the typhoon had reached its peak with winds now blowing from the north-northwest that measured 150 miles an hour. Ships initially grounded were blown out to sea again and dragged back across the beach. More collisions occurred. Gigantic waves swamped the smaller vessels and engulfed the larger ones. Liberty ships lost their propellers, while men who were aboard them were washed off into the sea as the decks were swept by gigantic waves.

On shore, the typhoon was also devastating the island of Okinawa. Twenty hours of torrential rain washed out all roads and ruined the island's store of rations and supplies. Aircraft were picked up and catapulted off the airfields. Quonset huts went sailing through the air. Metal hangars were ripped to shreds. The tent cities ceased to exist. Almost the entire food supply was blown away.

The Americans on the island had nowhere to go except into caves, trenches, or ditches, because pieces of board, sections of galvanized iron, and other materials were being hurled through the air at speeds greater than 100 miles an hour. The storm raged over the island for hours and then slowly headed out to sea. Then it doubled back --- and hit the island again!

Finally, two days later, when it had run itself out, the men crawled out of their holes to count the losses. All aircraft had been destroyed. All power was gone, and all communication with it. Supplies were non-existent.

Commanding General Joseph Stillwell of the Tenth Army called for B-29s to come in, because there was no other way to move people and to take the many injured to hospitals off the island. The toll in ships was staggering: 270 were sunk, grounded, or damaged; 53 were in too heavily damaged a state to be repaired. Of the remaining 90, the Navy decided only ten were worth salvaging.

According to Samuel Elliott Morrison, the noted naval historian, Typhoon Louise, as it was called, was the most furious and most lethal storm encountered by the U.S. Navy in its history. Hundreds of Americans were killed, injured, or missing. Hundreds of ships were sunk or severely damaged, and the island of Okinawa was in havoc.

Surprisingly, few people then or even now have made the connection between the planned invasion of Japan and the fleets of ships that would have been in exactly the same place, in the seas off Okinawa, at exactly the same time the typhoon enveloped the area. And by October 1, the date the invasion had been planned to start, the classified documents, with all the maps and detailed plans for the invasion, had already been crated up, classified, and shipped to the National Archives. Few people have looked at them --- until now.

In the aftermath of the storm and with war becoming a fading memory, few people would concern themselves with the plans for invading Japan. Anyhow, the invasion had been rendered unnecessary by the advent of the Atomic Age. But, had there been no atomic bombs dropped on Hiroshima and Nagasaki, a million Japanese voices would probably have been raised in thanksgiving once again to their Shinto gods for deliverance a second time by the divine wind they had named "Kamikaze" centuries earlier.

Now, whenever one is inclined to bewail or decry the use of those two nuclear bombs that were dropped on Hiroshima and Nagasaki, I hope they will reflect on what might have been the fate of the hundreds of thousands of Americans who would have been ordered to sea to invade the Japanese home islands at just the time that killer typhoon struck. Moreover, that typhoon would have destroyed the invasion force, and America could have subsequently lost the war.

It was the use of two --- just two! --- bombs that saved the U.S. invasion force from destruction. And why would it have taken so many men to invade Japan? Because by mid-1945, the U.S. Navy had had considerable experience with invasion tactics from the sea, and it knew, from Tarawa, Iwo Jima, and many other bloody island battlegrounds, what it would take to establish a beachhead and overwhelm a defending force.

Certainly the use of nuclear weapons ended the war without the enormous loss of American and Australian lives that an invasion would have meant, but there are many persons today, mostly intellectuals and anti-war sympathizers, who believe the Pacific War could have been stopped merely by the threat of a nuclear bomb or by a demonstration in some unoccupied area.

With respect to the actual use of an atomic bomb on Hiroshima, the anti-nuclear position is one of outrage. It also goes deeper than this one action. The Allied bombing of Dresden, Germany, is deplored, but not the German bombing of Coventry in England! Opponents express horror at the devastating fire-bombing of Tokyo (there were actually more deaths there than at Hiroshima), but they say nothing about the Rape of Nanking by the Japanese army in 1937, where 250,000 Chinese civilians were slaughtered within a few days.

Perhaps in a chapter on nuclear weapons and nuclear war, it isn't proper to mention the German campaign to exterminate Jews, the brutality against civilians and soldiers alike carried out by both sides on the Eastern Front in the Second World War, or the fierceness and bestiality Japan practiced on conquered people in the Pacific. Of course, it's not pleasant to write of such things, but they occurred, and it was largely because of them that the atomic bomb was developed in the first place and was used.

Many anti-war intellectuals appear to be Europe-oriented and fail to grasp the terrible brutality and ferocity of the war in the Pacific. To them, apparently, once the war in Eueope was ended, the defeat of Japan was essentially accomplished and diplomacy could finish the job.

Another apparent belief is that little thought was given to use of the bomb or to target selection. For example, McGeorge Bundy, one of the spokesmen for this position, said in his book, Danger and Survival (Page 74):

"We have seen the incompleteness of the examination in the Interim Committee, and the only other high-level discussion we know about was still more limited."

How did Bundy know? He even misunderstood the mission of the Interim Committee. It was made up of nine civilians appointed by President Truman on recommendation of Secretary of War Henry L. Stimson to draft postwar legislation, draw up news releases, and advise on steps needed to prepare the future handling of atomic energy in the U.S.

It was not part of their charge to recommend whether to use the atomic bomb against Japan. That was a decision for the military and for the Commander in Chief. Nevertheless, the Interim Committee set up a scientific advisory panel to consider whether a demonstration of the bomb should be conducted or a warning issued before actual use. The panel consisted of Arthur Compton, Enrico Fermi, Ernest Lawrence, and Robert Oppenheimer.

Fully aware of the feelings of some scientists, expressed in the Szilard letter and the Franck proposal, that a demonstration should be conducted before use but also knowledgeable about the nature of the enemy, the scientific panel concluded that:

"...We can propose no technical demonstration likely to bring about an end to the war; we see no acceptable alternative to direct military use."

The decision was not reached lightly. Moreover, the scientific panel and the Interim Committee knew that the battle for Okinawa (starting point for any invasion of the Japanese home islands), which began April 1, 1945, and took three months, cost the lives of 12,000 Americans, 110,000 Japanese troops, and 75,000 civilians, a grand total of 197,000 lives --- more than died at Hiroshima.

Even so, this high toll was believed to be only a fraction of the casualties expected in an invasion of the Japanese homeland. It was estimated that 36 American divisions would ultimately be required --- 1,532,000 men and women --- and the casualties would be heavy. Heavy on both sides, that is.

Against the background of experience in the Pacific, including, besides Okimawa, the enormous losses of military personnel at Guadalcanal, Tarawa, and Iwo Jima, the prospect of bringing the war to a close without invading Japan itself made both military and moral good sense. For anyone to believe now that it could have been ended with negotiation or a non-lethal demonstration --- remember we were negotiating with Japanese emissaries at a very high level when the Pearl Harbor attack took place --- defies facts and smacks of Monday morning quarterbacking at its worst.

It is always possible to play the "what if?" game with historical events, but is that anything more than an empty intellectual exercise? The game can also be played this way:

- What if there had not been so much negotiation (read that "appeasement") with Hitler?
- What if Germany had succeeded in building an atomic bomb?
- What if Britain had had the atomic bomb?
- What if the Soviet Union had produced an atomic bomb before the U.S.?

Would Germany, Britain, or the old Soviet Union have behaved as the U.S. did and

offered to put the technology under international control? There has <u>never</u> been a nation like the U.S.! There never was a country before the Second World War nor has there been one since that has done so much to help its defeated enemies. And no amount of "what if?" can change that.

In discussing the targeting of Japanese cities, Bundy

conveniently did not point out that cities have always been targets in war. Nor did he seem to realize that the cities selected for nuclear attack and approved by the Target Committee were chosen carefully for their military significance and because they had not already been hit by the Air Force in incendiary raids or with conventional bombs.

When Kyoto was disallowed on the insistence of Secretary Stimson and backed up by President Truman, General Leslie R. Groves made sure that it stayed on the list so that it would not be subject to conventional air raids. That Kyoto was spared any bombing at all was due to Groves' action (Pages 275-276 of his memoirs):

"About six weeks or so after Mr. Stimson refused to approve Kyoto, I suddenly realized that there was a danger that the Air Force might remove it from the list of proscribed cities. I spoke to (Air Force General) Arnold, who promptly saw to it that Kyoto remained on the reserved list and that the Air Force Command on Okinawa was also notified. If we had not recommended Kyoto as an atomic target, it would not, of course, have been reserved and most likely would have been seriously damaged, if not destroyed, before the war ended."

Because it bears on the important question of morality in war, I have one last comment on positions Bundy articulated, reflecting the opinion of the anti-nuclear camp. In the historical section of his book, he wrote (Page 96):

"Was not the nuclear weapon in and of itself morally and politically different from firebombs and blockades?"

And this: "Was there not also a political imperative to set an example of restraint?"

Surely he couldn't have been serious about "restraint" in the midst of war!

As for "morally and politically different," I can only ask: Different from what? From machine-gun bullets? Flesh-tearing shrapnel? Mustard gas? Nerve gas? Flame throwers? Anti-personnel mines? All of these and many, many more kill people, soldiers, and civilians alike. That is their purpose. The atomic bomb is only enormously more efficient.

Now, about the "imperative to set an example of restraint," the U.S. has tried that twice. The first was with the "mutual" test ban of 1958-61. Let's see what happened. On August 22, 1958, President Eisenhower announced that the U.S. was prepared, "....unless testing is resumed by the Soviet Union, to withhold further testing ... for a period of one year."

The unilateral moratorium began October 31, the day test-ban negotiations were scheduled to start in Geneva. Despite concerted efforts by the Eisenhower administration throughout 1959, the U.S. delegation in Geneva was unable to r each agreement with the Soviets on the terms of a test treaty.

Finally, it was agreed mutually to ban all tests. President Kennedy supported the ban, and all U.S. weapons work, including research, remained on hold. Then, without consultation, the U.S.S.R. announced on August 30, 1961, its intention to resume testing. The first test occurred the next day, on September 1, 1961, and was followed by a series of tests that continued until August, 1963.

The Soviet program consisted of about 100 tests in the atmosphere, an unknown number underground, and several at very high altitudes. In those two years, the Soviets conducted very complex weapons system tests involving previously emplaced missiles and radars, all of which required long preparation. The typical lead time for preparing a test is six to 18 months.

The U.S.S.R. conducted more tests above one megaton than the U.S. had in its entire history, a total of about 300. Clearly, the Soviets used the voluntary two-year test ban to prepare for its extensive weapons tests. The U.S. lost its lead in nuclear weaponry at that time. So where was the "imperative to practice restraint"?

The second example of self-restraint was imposed by President Carter when he announced unilaterally in 1977 that the U.S. would refrain from reprocessing fuel from nuclear power plants. The ostensible purpose was to curb proliferation --- for example, to reduce the likelihood that plutonium could be recovered from spent reactor fuel, refined, and used for weapons.

The expectation was that, if the U.S. denied itself the use of this valuable fuel (in other words, used self-restraint), other nations would do likewise. Of course, they didn't. Other nations are, in fact, reprocessing their fuel, and the only thing the U.S. got from this self-restraint was (a) loss of its leadership in the civilian power field and concomitantly loss of its ability to influence nuclear affairs, and (b) loss of its pre-eminent position in the multimillion-dollar international civilian nuclear fuels business. So much for self-restraint.

CHAPTER 4
NUCLEAR ARMS CONTROL AND TEST BANS

In this chapter, Dr. Ray brought her firsthand knowledge of nuclear-arms production to bear, with special emphasis on her strong opposition to test bans and their adverse effect on the U.S. nuclear program and the false sense of security the bans provide.

***

Regardless of what has happened in the past and the apparent political changes in what was once the U.S.S.R and throughout Eastern Europe, there is still good reason to maintain caution, militarily, in dealing with the "new" Russia. In spite of its many welcome overtures toward the West, Russia continues to be our main adversary in terms of nuclear power and capability.

Whatever some observers might say with reference to nuclear nations like China, India, Pakistan, and Middle Eastern nations, it remains clear that Russia continues to upgrade and modernize its strategic nuclear capabilities.

In the meantime, arms experts, disarmament officials, church organizations, citizen groups, and diverse governmental leaders keep calling for an end to nuclear arms. In an opinion survey reported in the Stanford Magazine (Spring, 1986), the attitudes of Stanford and Harvard University graduates were compared to those of the American population at large. According to the author, Florence Shelly, Americans overwhelmingly favored an emphasis on negotiating nuclear disarmament, rather than expanding the nation's nuclear arsenal, 87 percent to 13.

Stanford and Harvard alumni declared even stronger support for disarmament, 93 percent to 7.

In March, 1983, President Reagan envisioned a world in which we would no longer have to depend on strategic nuclear weapons to prevent nuclear war, and the Soviet leader at the time, Mikhail Gorbachev, in an article entitled, "If You Want Peace, Work for It," published in the Moscow News (No. 15, April 13, 1986), said, in part:

"Conclusion of a treaty to halt nuclear explosions between the Soviet Union and the United States would have a tremendous, real importance, because it would obstruct the sophistication of nuclear weapons and the development of new types thereof."

So what's wrong with a nuclear test ban? In view of all the evidence of widespread longing for a world free from the threat of nuclear war, why not take one step toward the elimination of nuclear weapons and ban the testing of bombs? Unfortunately, there is a great deal wrong with this most appealing notion.

The assumption that testing is solely or even primarily for the purpose of adding still more weapons to existing arsenals is simplistic and wrong. Test-ban proposals are always aimed at the U.S. and Russia, yet China, France, and several other countries possess nuclear arms or are on the verge of possessing them, as well as developing delivery systems. Most of these nations have stated unequivocally that they will not be bound by a test ban and will continue testing. To believe that only Russia and the U.S. should be restrained is like believing that one can be slightly pregnant.

Calls for a nuclear test ban ignore the fact that for more than a half century, nuclear deterrence has worked. No nuclear warheads have been detonated in battle, and the nuclear superpowers, despite all the tensions and misunderstandings that plague their relationship, have averted nuclear war.

Calls for a ban on nuclear testing overlook the many different reasons for conducting tests. The world has changed mightily since 1945 and the size and nature of the nuclear threat has also changed. Deterrence, which requires the maintenance of a credible stockpile, has responded to those changes and to developments in technology.

Nuclear weapons of different size and character, depending upon the needs of the time, have been developed. For example, in the 1950s, modernization of the nuclear arsenal generally meant bigger bombs. In the 1960s, the total destructive potential was four times as great as it is today.

Continued modernization over the past 40 years or so has resulted in warheads that are smaller, more compact, incorporate less fissionable materials, are safer both for handling and transportation, have reduced fallout, and are designed specifically for military targets, not civilian populations.

Today's nuclear weapons are not "just as indiscriminate," as is unfortunately too often implied; but they are more powerful than the Hiroshima-type bomb that was used to end the Second World War in the Pacific. Testing has made the improvements possible.

So why should we still test? Aside from the important fact that we have not reached the end of our knowledge, there is still much to learn about the nature of nuclear explosives, their effects, and how to control them. Other reasons relate to national security and safety. We should go on testing in order to:

- Continue modernizing and improving nuclear explosives for existing weapons systems.
- Prove the research and development undertaken for new and better weapons for defensive purposes.
- Maintain the reliability of deployed weapons, as well as those in the nuclear stockpile.

- Investigate the effect of nuclear explosives on military communications and other systems.
- Increase understanding of the physical phenomena of nuclear explosions.

Further explanation is in order. It should be stressed that to improve or modernize existing weapons means to make them smaller, safer, more tamperproof, and more sparing or conservative in the use of nuclear materials. It means reducing radioactive fallout or debris. And it means getting away from weapons of mass destruction, focusing effort on weapons designed specifically for military, not generalized or civilian, targets.

The notion that nuclear warheads are exclusively weapons of total and indiscriminate destruction is erroneous but firmly implanted in the public mind. Forgotten is the fact that in the Second World War, more civilians died in the fire-bombing of Tokyo than in the atomic blast at Hiroshima, as I detailed in the preceding chapter. I also cited the example of Dresden. These examples should not be interpreted as condoning the use of either fire-bombs or nuclear explosives, but only to put into perspective, without hysteria, some pertinent facts on destructiveness.

Modern nuclear weapons incorporate explosive materials that are less susceptible to accidental detonation than earlier versions. They permit reduced radiation levels for nearby personnel, and they incorporate unique safeguards to prevent accidental or unauthorized use. All these improvements require new weapon designs and these designs must be tested.

Nuclear weapons exist. They are a reality. They cannot be wished away, no matter how devout and sincere those wishes may be. And, since they exist, there is a corollary responsibility to make certain they are as safe, controllable, and reliable as humanly possible. This requires research and development, of which testing is an essential and indispensable component.

Moreover, for nuclear deterrence to be credible, we must know with certainty that the weapons will work as planned if called upon to do so. We cannot afford any "paper tigers" in the stockpile. But there's the rub. The problem is simply this: Nuclear weapons are very complex devices that are perishable. They deteriorate in time and become unreliable, inoperable, or function differently from the way they were designed. The estimate is that the reliable life of a nuclear warhead probably does not exceed 20 years.

For nuclear weapons, it is not necessarily a matter of "wearing out." They are required to operate only once. There is essentially no wear except for that associated with handling and transport. But like some household appliances or automobiles that have been stored for several years unused in a family's basement or garage, they may be found on close inspection to have deteriorated into an unusable condition.

This susceptibility to deterioration tends to be much higher for nuclear weapons than for other equipment, partly because weapons design must be determined mainly by the desired weapons performance and by safety considerations, rather than by demands for resistance to deterioration.

Certain chemically reactive materials, such as uranium, plutonium, high explosives, and plastics are inherently required in nuclear weapons. The fissile materials are subject to corrosion. Plastic bonded high explosives and other plastics tend to decompose over time.

Deterioration can take various forms. Some materials or portions of them can dissociate into simpler substances. Gases given off by one substance can migrate to another region of the weapon and react chemically there. One potential source of vapor is the thermonuclear fuel, lithium deuteride, which can react with water vapor and release hydrogen gas. Materials in the warhead electrical system, such as insulators, batteries, capacitors, and lubricants can produce effluents that can migrate to the nuclear explosive portion of the weapon.

Corrosion can create fissures and perforation that would have undesirable effects on operation. Mechanical components may have unacceptable friction introduced by corrosion products that flake off the surface. Vibration and other movements of the weapons can distribute these flakes like dust to locations where they could hamper the weapons' operation.

The characteristics of high explosives can change with time. Materials can creep and become distorted. Vital electrical components can change, and circuits can operate or become shorted. Some changes can obviously cause a weapon to dud; other changes can be more subtle and their effect on weapon performance can be difficult to predict ---without testing. All of these kinds of deterioration have been experienced with one or another weapon system in the stockpile.

U.S. practice has been to monitor the nuclear stockpile closely in order to detect deterioration at an early stage. Monitoring requires a sample inspection of each weapon type. It's not so easy as it may seem, since inspection requires disassembly to inspect the internal components. Disassembly is not a simple matter of undoing some bolts and screws to separate the various parts, because U.S. nuclear warheads are brazed, welded, and cemented together.

To disassemble a modern weapon is to destroy it. Many portions have to be machined apart. Few of the components could be reassembled and used again in a rebuilt weapon.

Generally, only the nuclear material is worth recovering, and it must be melted down and re-fabricated. If deterioration is found during this inspection process, it might require redesign to avoid the problem. Any design change introduces some degree of uncertainty, which may need to be resolved by a nuclear test.

If the warhead requires replacement by a different type, the replacement warhead will need various certification tests in its new role. It will also require non-nuclear operational tests, which also would be prohibited under most test-ban proposals.

Under a ban on testing, the U.S. would have no effective means to rehabilitate its stockpiled weapons. Testing is essential to maintaining our deterrent capacity.

Those who propose and support a nuclear test ban usually include the words "mutual" and "verifiable." In reality, a test ban could be neither. If that statement sounds overly pessimistic, consider that it springs from recognition of fundamental cultural differences between the Soviets and Americans and from events of the past 40 years.

We have already seen what happened during the "mutual" test ban of 1961-63. Practices we would view as unacceptable or even illegal may be treated by Russia as being allowable within the context of specified agreements.

It is fair to say that, while the U.S. observed the test moratorium and refrained even from research and development on improved weapons systems, the Soviet Union (and now Russia) used the device of a moratorium to conceal its preparations for the world's largest, most extensive, and best planned series of tests searching for improved nuclear weapons technology.

Russia can protest that, technically, it did not break the moratorium, because it did not actually conduct any tests during that period. But it made all the preparations necessary to execute a great many tests within a month of starting up.

When cultural differences between two peoples like the Russians and the Americans are so broad, how can one negotiate a concept like fairness or trust --- as the moratorium requires? Thus far, the two nations have divergent views about what should be the narrow letter of the agreement or the broader spirit.

The problems of reaching a "mutual" agreement, with safeguards that ensure the same perceptions on both sides, have proved insurmountable so far, despite strenuous effort by well intentioned negotiators. It should also be remembered that the Russians deployed their SS-20s during the months of negotiating, _while we were discussing with them whether SS-20s should be deployed at all!_ Once again, we awoke to find that what we were debating was an accomplished fact.

As for a "verifiable" test ban, verification of the destruction of certain weapons --- for example, intermediate range missiles --- is relatively easy, whereas verification of compliance with a test ban is one of the most difficult issues to understand, and one of the most important.

In principle, Russia has agreed to voluntary test-site inspection, but, in fact, it has demanded that the U.S. (and any other nation) be required to produce extensive seismic proof before consideration of a request for on-site inspection. Should the Russians conduct a secret test, the conclusive evidence we are least likely to have is seismic.

True, earth disturbances, such as earthquakes and underground nuclear tests, transmit a number of different shock waves through the earth and along its surface. These can be detected by sensitive instruments.

True, the pattern of "body waves" and "surface waves" differ somewhat between an earthquake and a nuclear explosion.

True, the pattern differences are easy to discern if the waves are received strong and clear, but they lose their identity at lower levels.

True, there is an international network of seismic receiving stations, but, whereas seismic events may be detected, it is often difficult to tell whether the cause is nuclear, chemical, or natural. And there are a large number of unidentified seismic events every year. Signals from many events are confused in the natural noise of the earth and many events simply escape detection.

It must also be acknowledged that, at present, tests are usually identified because of their known location near a test site or because of other identifying information. Tests conducted in hard rock are more easily identified than those detonated in soft earth, and it makes a big difference whether the test takes place above or below the water table. Shifting the test to previously unused areas of different geologic composition or into seismically active regions would confuse or make accurate seismic detection much more difficult and uncertain.

Finally, tests can be camouflaged in real earthquakes, multiple detonations can be designed to simulate earthquakes, and nuclear explosions can be set off in large "decoupling" cavities, such as salt domes, and even contained in large steel spheres.

The U.S. would find it hard to detect such tests and, even if detected, would have much greater difficulty identifying them. Even if the U.S. should discover what it believed to be a covert Russian test, it would be hard to pinpoint the exact location and to provide sufficient proof to persuade a world which did not wish to see violations that a violation has already occurred.

What remedy would be available to the U.S. if Russia refused to acknowledge its violation and also refused to permit on-site inspection? As long as Russia insists that on-site inspection is essentially voluntary, on a case-by-case basis, and requires seismic evidence to support an inspection request, non-seismic intelligence would be of limited value to enforce a comprehensive test-ban treaty.

In an effort to break the verification deadlock, the U.S. has developed a new technical method called CORTEX that is a fast, accurate system for measuring yields of underground explosives. The technique uses a coaxial cable, located either in the same hole as the nuclear device or emplaced in a nearby parallel "satellite" hole.

Precise measurements of the length of the cable are made by timing the return of low-energy electrical pulses sent down to every 10 to 90-millionths of a second. When the nuclear device is detonated, a shock wave emanates through the ground, crushing and therefore shortening the cable. The rate at which the cable length changes is a measure of the propagation rate of the explosive shock wave through the ground, which, in turn, is a measure of the yield of the nuclear explosion.

The CORTEX system has been used in hundreds of tests in the U.S. and has been described to the Russians. Offers to cooperate and share the system were made in September, 1984; February, 1985, and March, 1986, when President Reagan invited Gorbachev to send Russian inspectors to the Nevada test site to witness an explosion. No response was received from the Russians.

Without clear and unambiguous safeguards, including guaranteed on-site verification --- issues that are still unresolved, despite years of effort --- a nuclear test ban is not in the best interests of the U.S., nor of the free world.

In any event, recall again that it was the detonation of just two bombs that brought the war in the Pacific to a close. Truly, it was not so much the killing of large numbers of people and destruction of many buildings in Hiroshima and Nagasaki that caused the Japanese government to accept the terms of surrender. No, the awesome truth is that the devastation in the Japanese cities was caused in an instant by only two bombs, one for each of the cities. And, also, a new element of warfare --- radiation --- had been introduced.

At this point, I am compelled to point out that, contrary to popular opinion, many people did, indeed, survive in both Hiroshima and Nagasaki, and both cities are large, bustling metropolises today. The devastation was not forever. Nor have there been any genetic effects, as determined by more than a half century of medical study. The only type of cancer to show some increased incidence is leukemia.

Much has been learned about radiation effects by the ongoing studies of the survivors. I point out these facts not to appear to condone nor to justify the use of atomic or another weapons, but only to set the record straight.

Suffice it to say that no person who is sane --- and especially no person who is both moral and sane --- is in favor of nuclear war. My purpose here is to try to encourage people to think clearly and realistically about nuclear weapons, and to think about nuclear war in moral terms so as to be better able to make rational decisions based on fact, not emotion.

***

Nuclear Warheads and Plutonium
In Nuclear Power Reactors

There is already enough irrationality about nuclear weapons. Some of it concerns what it takes to make a nuclear warhead and whether this can be accomplished by using the plutonium that is produced in the fuel of civilian electricity-generating nuclear power plants.

Recall that the Plutonium-239 that is produced in an operating reactor is soon converted into "reactor grade" Plutonium-240. Now, Plutonium-240 happens to be a prolific emitter of neutrons. In a power plant, the fuel typically remains in the reactor for three years. As a consequence, something like 30 percent of the plutonium produced comes out as Plutonium-240. If this material is used in a bomb, the Plutonium-240 produces a steady show of 2 million neutrons per second, which on an average would reduce the power of the explosion tenfold but might cause a fizzle.

To understand why this is, it is necessary to know how a plutonium bomb works.

There are two stages in its operation. First, there is an implosion in which the plutonium is blown together and powerfully compressed by chemical explosives which surround it. Then there is the explosion, in which neutrons are introduced to start a rapidly escalating chain reaction of fission processes, which release an enormous amount of energy very rapidly to blow the system apart.

All of this takes place within a millionth of a second, and the timing must be precise. If the explosion phase starts much before the implosion process is completed, the power of the bomb is greatly reduced. In fact, one of the principal methods that's been considered for defending against nuclear bombs is to shower them with neutrons to start the explosion early in the implosion process, thereby causing the bombs to fizzle. For the bomb to work properly, it is important that no neutrons come upon the scene until the implosion process approaches completion.

In short, a bomb made of "reactor grade plutonium" has a relatively low explosive power and is highly unreliable. It is also difficult to design and construct.

A much better bomb fuel is "weapons grade plutonium," produced by leaving the material in a reactor for only about 30 days to maximize the amount of Plutonium-239. This reduces the amount of time for Plutonium-240 and hence the number of neutrons showering the bomb by tenfold.

A power reactor could be used to produce weapons grade plutonium by removing the fuel for reprocessing every 30 days, but this would be highly impractical, because fuel removal requires about a 30-day shutdown. In addition, the fuel for a power reactor is very expensive to fabricate, because it must operate in a very compact geometry at high temperature and pressure to produce the high-temperature, high-pressure steam needed to generate electricity.

That's why it is much more practical to build a separate plutonium production reactor designed not to generate electricity but rather to provide easy and rapid fuel removal. The fuel is cheaper to fabricate, because the reactor operates at low temperature and normal pressure. Also, it can use natural uranium, rather than the very expensive enriched uranium needed to power reactors.

Another alternative would be to use a research reactor, one designed to provide radiation for research applications, rather than to generate electricity. More than 45 nations now have research reactors, and in about 25 or so of them there is a capability of producing enough plutonium to make one or more bombs every two years. Research reactors are usually designed with lots of flexibility and space, so it would not be difficult to use them for plutonium production, whereas it is hard to use power reactors.

A power plant for generating nuclear electricity is large and highly complex, with most of the size and complexity due to reaction operation at very high temperature and pressure, to the need for the production and handling of steam and the equipment for generation and distribution of electricity. It would be impossible to keep construction or operation of such a plant secret.

It is also true that only a few of the most technologically advanced nations are capable of constructing one. A production or research reactor, on the other hand, can be small and unobtrusive. It has no high pressure or temperature, no steam, and no electricity generation or distribution equipment.

Many nations have or could easily acquire the capability for constructing one, and the entire project could probably be carried out in secret. There would be no compulsion to submit to outside inspection.

In view of all these considerations, it would be completely illogical for a nation bent on making nuclear weapons to obtain a power reactor for that purpose. It would be much cheaper, faster, and easier to obtain a plutonium production reactor; the plutonium it produces would make much more powerful and reliable bombs with less effort and expense.

But Plutonium-239 can also be obtained by utilizing isotope separation capability. At least nine nations now have facilities for isotope separation, and others would have little difficulty in acquiring the technology. A plant for this purpose, costing $20 million to $200 million, could provide the fuel for two to 20 bombs per year and could be constructed and put into operation in three to five years. The product material would be very easy to convert into excellent bombs, much easier than making a plutonium bomb, even with weapons grade plutonium. Finally, the easiest way to acquire an atomic bomb is to steal or buy one!

The main point here is that the U.S. position of denying reprocessing and subsequent use of the plutonium resource to ourselves in no way affects either weapons proliferation or decisions by other countries to reprocess for their own fuel benefit.

***

The Question of Nuclear Terrorism

What about the issue of terrorists stealing plutonium? For whatever purpose?

First, we're really dealing with relatively small amounts of material. Can we protect it?

If all our electricity were derived from breeder reactors fueled by plutonium, the quantities of plutonium involved would still not be very large. All of the plutonium in a breeder reactor would fit inside a household refrigerator and all the plutonium existing at any one time in the U.S. would fit into a home living room. The great majority of it would be inside reactors or in spent fuel, where the intense radiation would preclude the possibility. As in the case of radioactive waste, the small quantities involved make very elaborate security measures practical.

There have been charges that all the security measures we've employed with armed guards would turn the U.S. into a police state. However, the total number of people required to safeguard plutonium would be only a small fraction of the number now used for security checking at airports to prevent hijacking of planes. That force has hardly given the nation a police-state character.

And what about terrorists using an armed attack against a power plant? Security measures make a direct onslaught most unlikely to succeed, and should terrorists gain entrance, how could they make off with the highly radioactive fuel? Perhaps, say the critics, they could use sophisticated weaponry from a hilltop and rupture the entire pressure vessel so as to "release this radioactivity."

The containment building is made of concrete 3.5 feet thick, with the steel reinforcement mesh so tightly woven that vibrators must be used to force the concrete through it before it hardens. That makes the walls much stronger than, for example, the rooms of the German submarine bases on the French Atlantic coast, which were bombed 'round the clock by the Allied Air Forces with "blockbuster" bombs, but withstood even direct hits.

But suppose an imaginary super-saboteur did have some mysterious missile that managed to blow a hole in the containment building. What next? Would he have a second missile to make the hole larger and a third to penetrate the remaining concrete structures inside the building ---- and a fourth to begin working on the steel pressure vessel?

Would he wait until the weather is just right so that the fruits of his labors are not dispersed harmlessly in the atmosphere? This does not yet ask all the questions, but the whole idea is too absurd to waste more space on.

The fact remains, nuclear weapons exist. They will not just "go away." Nor will any other weapon. But they may be held in check --- as they have the past half century. The history of weaponry is a litany of the development of means to kill people ever more efficiently.

Weapons have gone from clubs to spears, bows and arrows to crossbows --- which the Catholic Church once tried to ban as being "inhuman" --- from gunpowder to cannon and artillery, to machine guns and automatic fire, to poison gas and napalm, tanks, airplanes, and nuclear explosives --- each more deadly than the ones before.

Yet, war has always been with us, and continues to this day.

CHAPTER 5
THE THEORY OF A "JUST WAR"

*F*or centuries, philosophers have argued the question: Is there such a thing as a "Just War"? In my conversations with Dr. Ray, she left no doubt about which side of the debate she favored. In fact, she has devoted many speeches and articles to the issue, as I have. Needless to say, I agree heartily with her viewpoint, expressed here. In addition, this chapter contains an alarming warnng from Dr. Ray for those who believe modern Russia is no longer a threat to the U.S. and to peace.

***

The 20th Century, particularly its second half, may well be remembered as the bloodiest in the history of civilized man. Untold millions have been killed in wars since 1945 --- wars that were sanctioned by the governments involved, and all of them fought with non-nuclear weapons.

Can we forget or overlook:
- The human slaughter when India and Pakistan separated?
- The bloodbaths in Indonesia, Rhodesia, Biafra, Angola, Ethiopia, Korea, Vietnam, Cambodia….?

- The recurring battles in the Middle East that have involved Iran, Iraq, Israel, Lebanon, Syria, and Egypt?
- The deaths in Afghanistan, Tibet, and the Ukraine?
- The unending bloodshed in Northern Ireland?
- The civil war in China and the blood bath in Beijing?
- The carnage in Central American nations?

Considering that, of the millions that have been slaughtered in wars since the end of the Second World War, not one has died from nuclear weapons, surely it is time to rethink the premise that the use of atomic bombs is the main threat or only instrument of mass destruction. It is time, also, to cease being mesmerized by nuclear weapons and to think, coolly and clearly, about other instruments of annihilation --- like fire-bombing, chemical warfare, and biological warfare.

Indeed, it is war itself that needs new and sober study. War, --- that uniquely human activity that sanctions the use of deadly force to kill human beings --- should be the real focus of attention. For those scholars so taken with the wickedness of nuclear weapons, I believe it would be instructive to review again the "Just War" theory put forward by St. Augustine in early Roman Catholic thought. The contributions to serious thinking on this subject by Aquinas and by Sir Thomas More should be explored in the light of modern realities.

For all of those who are deeply concerned about the morality of nuclear weapons, a review of Hugo Grotius' (1583-1645) masterpiece, "The Law of War and Peace," would be most illuminating.

Most people express horror and revulsion at the ravages of modern war, but the fact is that human history is a chronicle of battles and conquerors, of the resolution of differences through armed conflict. Indeed, the history of the human race is a recitation of one war after another, all intended to resolve unsolvable crises between peoples. In this context, nuclear weapons, along with other means of mass annihilation --- chemical and biological weapons, for example --- are not all that different from what man has been doing to man since the beginning of time.

No one makes the historical point more clearly than James W. Child in his Nuclear War, The Moral Dimension (Transaction Books):

"Some peoples," he reminds us, "have made war their primary cultural activity, or source of livelihood, or both. The Yanomamo of the Orinoco Valley in Venezuela live to fight. War and plunder (more often than not visited upon noncombatants) were central to the tribal existence of the Mongols, the Norse raiders, and numerous American Indian tribes."

Of more relevance to our purposes, total war --- defined as the obliteration of whole societies and the enslavement or slaughter of whole people --- did not arrive with the nuclear weapon or even with the strategic bomber. It is literally as old as recorded history. Sargon of Akkad, for example, conducted strategic devastation through Mesopotamia around 714 B.C.

If one accurately captures the essence of war in history, it is not the battlefield but the siege and sack of cities and the devastation of the countryside; it is total war carried out upon civilians.

The Second Punic War (218-201 B.C.) matched two of the greatest generals of the ancient world, Hannibal and Scipio Africanus. The battles they fought are still studied in military schools. Less often remembered is the horrible devastation that resulted in Southern Italy, the locus of most of their campaigns, devastation that resulted from the marching armies, rather than the historic battles. Some claim that 40 percent of the civilian population was killed or died of hunger or disease in the 17 years of the war.

Genghis Khan (1162?-1227), one of the greatest conquerors of all time, quite consciously used terror to prompt surrender. In one particularly brutal campaign, he attempted to slaughter the entire population of the Khorezin Empire of Persia. He did not quite succeed, although millions must have died and scores of cities and towns were completely destroyed in the process.

Desmond Seward, in his excellent book, The Hundred

Years' War: The English in France, 1337-1453, gives us a frightening account of strategic devastation on a smaller scale, but one which is completely characteristic of military campaigns throughout history --- and, of course, closer to our own heritage than the examples already cited:

"On 13 July 1346, the English armada landed at La Hogue, on the north of the Cherbourg Peninsula.... The following day, the King launched a *chevauchee* through the Cotentin, deliberately devastating the rich countryside, his men burning mills and barns, orchards and haystacks, smashing wine vats, tearing down and setting fire to the thatched cabins of the villagers, whose throats they cut together with those of their livestock.

"One may presume that the usual atrocities were perpetrated on the peasants --- the men were tortured to reveal hidden valuables, the women suffered multiple rapes and sexual mutilation, those who were pregnant were disemboweled. Terror was an indispensable accompaniment to every *chevauchee* and Edward obviously intended to wreak the maximum 'dampnum' --- the medieval term for that total war which struck at an enemy King through his subjects...."

The chronicle continues: "On 26 July, King Edward's army reached Caen, larger than any town in England, apart from London, and soon stormed their way through the bridge gate. When the garrison surrendered, the English started to plunder, rape, and kill, 'for the soldiers were without mercy.' The desperate inhabitants then began to throw stones, wooden beams, and iron bars from the rooftops down into the narrow streets, killing more than 500 Englishmen. Edward ordered the entire population to be put to the sword and the town burnt, 'and there were done in the town many evil deeds, murders, and robberies' --- although Godefroi d'Harcourt persuaded the King to rescind his order. The sack lasted three days, and 3,000 townsmen died."

And so goes the grim tale throughout Edward's entire campaign in France.

Closer to our own time, it is estimated that in the Thirty

Years' War (1618-1648), as much as 40 percent of the population of Germany was wiped out either directly by siege or by strategic devastation with its consequent disease and hunger. Reports of starvation and cannibalism were not uncommon.

What was almost certainly the greatest human cost ever expended in human conflict before the dawn of the 20th Century is almost unknown in the West. In the middle of the 19th Century, China was wracked by a series of revolutions and outbursts of civil violence on a scale never seen anywhere before. They lasted from 1850 until 1878. The cost in lives can never be known within even a broad approximation, but it was vast. The worst outbreak, called the Taiping Revolution, lasted from1850 to 1864. It has been estimated that 40 million people died there, perhaps 10 percent of the entire population of China,. Much of this monumental human cost resulted from the conscious policies of both the rebels and the Imperial Manchu armies as they killed civilians and induced starvation by strategic devastation.

In general, wars throughout history were characterized by armies marching from siege to siege and laying waste to the countryside along the way. Moreover, one is constantly struck while reading in primary historical sources just how casually such brutality was accepted.

Hugo Grotius did as much as anyone to try to civilize and humanize warfare. Nonetheless, in his <u>The Law of War and Peace</u>, he blithely comments that after a city falls to siege, the commander *ought* to turn it over to his troops for three days of plunder (always unavoidably attended by rapes and killings). "It is, after all," he assures us, "a conventional law of war, honored throughout history." He was quite correct, of course. And, besides, he continues, it is their due! Just three days though, no more!

Quite simply, most wars in history have been total wars waged without quarter against combatants and noncombatants alike, with the level of destruction limited only by the means available. Sometimes this viciousness and brutality was part of the conscious use of terror; sometimes it was completely with rational purpose. Whether purposeful or not, it occurred over and over throughout history.

Although the glorification of war is as ancient as Homer and the Old Testament, there is also a long and honorable tradition of pacifism. While this has prevailed among some small groups --- for example, the Quakers, Amish, and Christians in Roman times --- it has never really succeeded to become a guiding philosophy among nations.

But there is another tradition, and this is the one I wish to explore. It's based on an appeal to morality and rationality. It's the "Just War" tradition. The "Just War" philosophy rejects the glorification of war but provides affirmative answers to two proud questions:

1. Are there ever any reasons that morally justify waging war?

2. Are there any means by which war can be waged morally?

These questions were first propounded in the Catholic Church when the Roman Empire was Christianized, and orderly life had to be protected from barbarians. St. Augustine was among the first to try to set the conditions by which Christians might be justified in fighting. St. Thomas Aquinas took up the problem and concluded that, to be justified, a war must be (1) waged by a properly constituted authority, for example a government; (2) waged in a just cause, for example, to repel an invasion, and (3) waged with a proper attitude, for example, the enemy must not be dehumanized.

Thomas More, fierce pacifist though he was, accepted these precepts for a "Just War."

It was Grotius who codified the legal ramifications of military campaigns. It was he who first discussed the treatment of prisoners and hostages, the rights of safe conduct, freedom of the seas, good faith in truces and treaties, treatment of noncombatants --- all of which have been incorporated in modern times into the Geneva Convention. His conclusion, like that of the Roman Catholic officials before him, was that there are some circumstances in which war is justified.

Bullies and evil do exist, but if war must be fought, it should be done without losing one's humanity. Can these concepts, *jus ad bellum* (justice in war), apply to the use of nuclear weapons?

The awesome destructive power of a strategic nuclear warhead would seem disproportionate to any reasonable political or military goal. But, contrary to popular belief, not all nuclear weapons are strategic. Fully 15 to 25 percent of the U.S. arsenal consists of small-yield, tactical warheads that can be directed toward targets that are specifically military in nature.

Few can support a premeditated first strike, and there is little question that we would reject the offensive use of nuclear weapons, but, considering the principles of "Just War," could we use nuclear weapons, specifically tactical ones, to defend ourselves?

Quite clearly, the primary purpose of a nuclear weapon is to remain unused. This is the paradox of deterrence --- the intention to remain unused. Is it a bluff? Without a firm, credible determination to use nuclear force, is the deterrent meaningful? In the face of this dilemma, some people urge nuclear disarmament, others an improved war-fighting capability. Which of these options is more compatible with "Just War" theory?

Let's try to look rationally at this dilemma and lay out five propositions:
1. We have an overwhelming, even a moral duty, to avoid nuclear war....
a. But it is not necessary to go to any length --- for example, at the cost of losing our liberty.
2. We must take all reasonable steps to avoid nuclear war....
a. This includes being strong enough in nuclear arms to deter --- and secure enough to survive an attack.
3. We have a moral right to fight with nuclear weapons if we are attacked by an enemy using nuclear weapons....

a. This is the right of self-defense.
4. We have a duty to minimize noncombatant casualties....
   a. This means using tactical, rather than strategic, warheads.
5. Within the bounds set out, if building a nuclear arsenal constitutes a threat, it is nevertheless moral to make a deterrent threat, for....
   a. "If one loses one's liberty, one is right to blame --- not so much the man who puts the fetters on as he who had the power to prevent it but did not use it." So said the Corinthian emissaries to Sparta in 426 B.C.

Their statement is true today. To maintain our liberty, we must project, credibly, the will to fight and the capacity to win.

Since the middle of the 20th Century, the United States has borne a heavy responsibility worldwide for preventing aggression and preserving liberty. In this regard, the U.S.S.R., now Russia, has not been helpful. It is possible, of course, that the Russians will embrace the "Just War" principles. It is even possible that they are no longer our main adversary; it is possible that they have undergone fundamental change, as first proclaimed by President Gorbachev; it is possible that Russia no longer seeks domination of the U.S., the West, and the world, and no longer works for total military superiority. Possible, yes, but not certain. The facts tell a different story.

Could it be that with its food supply collapsing and basic consumer goods, like soap and shoes, in severe shortage, its entire economy in crisis, the captive nations of Eastern Europe now free, and others from Georgia to Latvia in revolt, that the old Soviet Union was accepting it all --- or was preparing for war? Could it be that by talking arms reduction, the Russians were lulling the West into a false sense of security? Could it be that the longstanding goal of driving a wedge between Europe and the U.S. was being achieved through reduction in the weapons that threatened Western Europe, while the modernization and upgrading of long-distance strategic arms proceeded apace? Against whom were the Russian ICBMs, submarines, long-range cruise missiles, etc., to be directed?

As pointed out by Cutshaw (Charles Q. Cutshaw, military analyst and chief of the Foreign Systems Division, U.S. Army), Gorbachev's announced reduction in troop strength and tanks was not a surprise. It was expected. The reductions covered older tanks and aircraft and had little effect on modernized, over-all Soviet military strength.

Also, none of the 500,000 troop reductions that were announced included career officers, noncommissioned officers or career enlisted men. They were the conscripts, who would depart when their two-year hitch ended. There would be fewer new conscripts. Every change in the Russian military pointed to a stronger, more lethal strategic force than had existed. The facts were, according to a 1989 report made public by Senator John McCain, a member of the Armed Services Committee:

"The Soviets are producing tanks at a faster rate under Gorbachev than they were under Brezhnev. Soviet tank production has increased from 2,600 annually in 1983 to 3,500 in 1968. U.S. tank production dropped during the same period from 1,200 tanks to 775. The Soviet tanks have armor and guns distinctly superior to the U.S. M-1 tank.

"The Soviets maintain a massive advantage in other armored vehicles, although production has dropped slightly. In 1983, a total of 5,500 vehicles was produced, compared to 5,250 in 1988. U.S. production was 1,000 vehicles in 1983 and 1,100 in 1988.

"In the important area of self-propelled artillery (rocket launchers, mortars, conventional missiles), Soviet production decreased from 1,600 weapons in 1983 to 1,550 in 1988. U.S. production went from 506 to 223.

"In the area of air weapons, the Soviets now deploy four fighter-bombers: The Su-24 Fencer, the Su-27 Flanker, the MIG-29 Fulcrum, and the MIG 31 Foxhound. The total payload delivery capability of this class of aircraft in missions within a combat radius of 500 kilometers increased by 70 percent from 1980 to 1988. In missions up to 1,000 km, the payload capability more than doubled in the same time frame.

In terms of production, the Soviets produced 950 fighters and fighter-bombers in 1983 and 700 in 1988. U.S. production rose from 400 aircraft to 550 in the same period.

"The trends in military helicopters are similar. The Soviets produced 600 in 1983 and 400 in 1988. U.S. production rose during the same period from 300 weapons to 375.

Both U.S. fighter production and helicopter production will decrease radically in 1989 because of defense cutbacks. The Advanced Tactical Fighter is being stretched out, and the AH-64 helicopter and Army Helicopter Improvement Program are being canceled. This left the U.S. without any production of state-of-the-art fighters and helicopters well into the mid-1990s.

The Soviets are widening their lead in fielded submarines; they produced ten submarines in 1983 and nine in 1988. U.S. submarine production averaged five per year during this time span. During the Gorbachev era, the Soviets produced 34 submarines, the United States only 15.

"From 1983 to 1988, the Soviet production of surface warships decreased from 11 to 9. U.S. production fell from 11 ships to three during this period.

"The Soviets continued to outproduce the U.S. in other nuclear systems. Despite Gorbachev's image as an advocate of arms control, Soviet production of ICBMs rose from 75 weapons in 1984 to 150 in 1988. U.S. production of the MX ranged from 11 to 26 per annum during the same period. During Gorbachev's tenure, the Soviets produced a total of 450 ICBMs, the United States only 56.

"The Soviets also produced greater numbers of nuclear bombers. They produced 35 aircraft in 1983 and increased this to 45 in 1988. U.S. production rose from zero to 22, but U.S. production was halted until the B-2 Stealth bomber was ready for production.

"The advantage the U.S. once had in cruise missiles is fast disappearing. Soviet production of long-range, sea-launched cruise missiles increased from 150 in 1983 to 300 in 1988. U.S. production rose from 40 to 280 in this same period.

Soviet production of short-range, sea-launched cruise missiles dropped slightly from 850 in 1983 to 800 in 1988, but improved in accuracy and performance. U.S. production dropped from 490 to 400 during this period."

In concluding his statement, Senator McCain observed: "The Soviets have pursued a different course than the U.S. (during Gorbachev's tenure). The U.S. is entering its fifth year of real cuts in defense spending. The disparity between Soviet and U.S. military equipment production in area after area is becoming so great that it raises serious questions about the long-term impact of the resulting gap on Western security."

Could it be that the Soviets were positioning themselves to be able to take from the West, by armed strength, the concessions, the credits, and economic advances they might not receive otherwise? Could they have military blackmail in mind? For what purpose did they continue to expand their military power?

Coupled with continued buildup and improvement in strategic weapons, including the installation of reactive armor on Soviet tanks, which has made the U.S. TOW Missiles obsolete and ineffective, the Soviets have the world's only operational ABM (anti-ballistic-missile) system. It is a two-layered defense, involving 100 launchers (the maximum permitted by the ABN Treaty); the U.S. has none. Although the ABM system currently protects Moscow only, there is evidence that the Russians are developing other ABM sites, a clear violation of the ABM Treaty.

While the U.S. struggles to keep its Strategic Defense Initiative (S.D.I.) research going, the Soviets are experimenting with laser beams, particle beams, and radio-frequency and microwave systems. These are being studied primarily as a means of destroying incoming rockets by damaging their electronics. Although all beam weapons kill people, too, the radio-frequency types are particularly nasty, since they destroy or damage nerve synapses. They can totally disable people over a distance of several kilometers, and they're portable enough to transport in trucks or aircraft.

The real danger we face today is a large, probably superior military force in a nation that is economically unstable and facing financial collapse. Our response appears to be probable dismantlement of our own military capability. The alternative to this dismal situation would be to support S.D.I. at a much enhanced level.

The type of technologies and scientific advances involved --- high-energy lasers, laser-welding, superconductivity, and new materials and new propulsion systems, to name just a few --- would also drive a real advance in industrial productivity.

The applications, both military and civilian, are legion. If the Apollo program returned $14 of real, non-inflationary wealth to the U.S. economy for every dollar spent on it (as determined by Chase Econometrics Associates in 1976), the S.D.I. program would do no less.

Military technology is undergoing revolutionary changes and Second World War-type battles will probably not be fought in the future. Real and perceived military strength in the 21st Century will be essentially in three areas --- electronics, space, and lasers. The U.S. has been and continues to be the pre-eminent leader in computers, sensors, and communications, including their miniaturization.

But our situation with respect to leadership in space is vacillating and uncertain. When we were contending worldwide with Great Britain, we insisted on freedom of the seas; today, when it remains Russian doctrine to dominate space, we should insist on freedom of space.

With respect to lasers and beam weapons, we have so far conceded the leadership to the Russians. If we do not pursue study of these highly precise weapons so as to know how to protect ourselves, as well as how to use them to protect ourselves from nuclear warheads --- and if the U.S. does not use its own technological ingenuity to develop and deploy defenses against the new technological weapons, then we will have lost all hope of maintaining a military balance with the Russians.

The facts --- not euphoria nor conjecture --- would indicate that the Russians have in mind something going beyond a "Just War." Is it reasonable to expect a "Just Peace"? Can hope and good intentions protect us?

CHAPTER 6
TIME FOR A NEW ENVIRONMENTAL POLICY

*D*r. *Ray and I were among the very few persons who pioneered the first environmental movement in the Pacific Northwest in the early 1950s. The movement gained adherents gradually and brought about many improvements in urban and rural living. But with the advent of Rachel Carson's inaccurate "Silent Spring" and the brash takeover by the militant, political environmental activists in the 1970s, Dr. Ray and I departed the movement and began warnings against excessive environmentalism and such myths as global warming and the ozone hole. This is her pronouncement on the issue, and it echoes my beliefs, as well.*

***

America --- and, in fact, the entire world --- is sorely in need of a new, sensible, and scientifically sound environment policy that recognizes the need for assigning priority status on all issues to human beings, not lower animals, birds, insects, trees, plants, or anything else. Anyone who assumes that I have a somewhat skeptical and irreverent attitude toward such popular environmental scenarios as "Global Warming" and "Ozone Depletion" is absolutely correct.

Yet it appears that a great many persons --- too many --- believe the earth must be saved from those two "dangers" and many more! Why? Well, because so many "experts" say so. But what is the evidence? What and where are the data that support these issues, and are there any contrary facts? They must be discussed.

First, global warming. The claim is that the earth is warming up and that it is human activity, burning fossil fuels, that increases the CO2 content of the atmosphere that is the cause. Moreover, the consequences of global heating are claimed to be disastrous, including changes in weather --- rainfall, agricultural crops, sea level, etc.

Before examining the evidence, let's pause and look back to a similar set of claims made back in the 1970s. Then the issue was not global warming but global cooling! It was widely believed by many climatologists at the time that a new ice age --- with catastrophic consequences --- was imminent.

An ice age, they said, "would result in droughts, a shorter growing season, and worldwide hunger at first, and later in extensive glaciation." Their commonly proposed solutions included a deliberate melting of polar ice, the enactment of strict pollution regulations, and the stockpiling of food. To quote some of them:

"The cooling has already killed hundreds of thousands of people in poor nations. It has already made food and fuel more precious, thus increasing the price of everything we buy. If it continues, and no strong measures are taken to deal with it, the cooling will cause world famine, world chaos, and probably world war, and this could all come by the year 2000." --- Lowell Ponte, "The Cooling," 1976.

"The facts have emerged, in recent years and months, from research into past ice ages. They imply that the threat of a new ice age must now stand alongside nuclear war as a likely source of wholesale death and misery for mankind." --- Nigel Calder, former editor of <u>New Scientist</u>, "In the Grip of a New Ice Age," <u>International Wildlife</u>, July, 1975.

"There are ominous signs that the earth's weather patterns

have begun to change dramatically and that these changes may portend a drastic decline in food production --- with serious political implications for just about every nation on earth." --- Peter Gwynne, Newsweek, April 28, 1975.

"According to the academy [National Academy of Sciences] report on climate, we may be approaching the end of a major interglacial cycle, with the approach of a full-blown 10,000-year ice age a real possibility ... with ice packs building up relatively quickly from local snowfall that ceases to melt from winter to winter." --- Science, March 1, 1975.

"The continued rapid cooling of the earth since World War II is also in accord with the increased global air pollution associated with industrialization, mechanization, urbanization, and an exploding population, added to a renewal of volcanic activity...." --- Reid Bryson, "Environmental Roulette," Global Ecology: Readings Toward a Rational Strategy for Man, John P. Holdren and Paul R. Ehrlich, editors, 1971.

"The sensitivity of climate was pointed up independently by a Soviet and an American scientist, who concluded that a permanent drop of only 1.6 to 2 percent in energy reaching the earth 'would lead to an unstable condition in which continental snow cover would advance to the Equator...[and] the oceans would eventually freeze,' according to a recent U.S. scientific advisory report." --- Samuel W. Matthews, "What's Happening to Our Climate?" National Geographic, November, 1976.

(All quotations are from "The Ice Age Cometh: Remembering the Scare of Global Cooling," by Anne J. Bray, Policy Review, Fall, 1991, pp. 82-84.)

How similar these warnings sound to what is being said today about global warming! Are our memories so short? Are they as serious and as frightening as the activists in these areas would have us believe? I think not. But let me explain why.

For more than 40 years, the American public has been subjected to a barrage of criticism about the way we live, about what we eat, about how we manufacture the materials that mark our incredibly productive society in the age of high technology, about how much and what kind of energy we use, and about how we handle the inevitable waste products of our activities.

More recently we've been told that we are destroying the earth and its capacity to support life. These scoldings include predictions of catastrophe, unless we make fundamental, unpleasant, and costly changes in the way we live. They have become a virtual litany of impending disaster. They have also become a crusade to "Save the Planet." The charges are very serious; the question is, are they right? What *is* the evidence that supports them, and is there contrary evidence?

With respect to global warming, there are two situations that are not in dispute:

First, the Earth and its atmosphere constitute a "greenhouse"; our air is a porous blanket. If that were not the case, our planet would respond to the sun's radiation the same as does the moon, whose temperature during the lunar day may reach +121 degrees F and drop to –270 degrees F during the lunar night. On Earth, roughly 30 percent of the incoming solar radiation is reflected back into space by the atmosphere, 20 percent is absorbed in the atmosphere, and 50 percent penetrates to the Earth's surface to cause warming. Of this latter, some fraction is reflected back as infra-red radiation, which in turn may be absorbed by certain constituents of air, the so-called "greenhouse gases." (Carbon dioxide, methane, hydrocarbons, and, above all, water vapor). Increase in the relative amount of any of these gases will, theoretically, result in elevated surface temperatures..

The theory is well established and well supported, by both theoretical and experimental evidence. There's only one problem --- the theory doesn't appear to work in so simple a cause-and-effect manner in nature. If it did, the Earth would have warmed 2 degrees to 4 degrees C over the past 100 years. It has not. At best, there might have been about 0.5C increase in temperature, but that took place before 1940, and there has been about the same amount of cooling since then. Temperature records taken in the Northern Hemisphere over the past century show no upward trend. Further:

- Analysis of 135 years of surface ocean temperatures taken by ships at sea shows no upward trend (Professor Reginald Newell, M.I.T.).
- Analysis of 10 years (1978-1988) of satellite measurements (TIROS II) taken continuously, day and night, over land and sea show no consistent change --- up or down. (published in Science).
- Analysis of certain plant species in the U.S.A. give an interesting picture; for example:

1. It used to be possible to grow citrus fruit in the Southeast region of America as far north as the Carolinas. Now, oranges will not ripen north of Orlando, Florida.
2. In Florida, there have been 24 "arctic breakouts"; that is, episodes of severe killing frosts in the past 30 years or so. There had been only six in the previous 50 years.
3. In 1990, the U.S. Department of Agriculture put out its first revised hardiness report for commercial crops since 1965. Taking temperature data from 14,500 measuring stations, the new maps show that the area in which crops can be grown without certain danger of a killing frost has moved 100 miles south in the past 50 or 60 years.

Such data should come as no surprise. The whole history of Planet Earth is one of weather and climate change. There have been warm years and there have been cold ones. There have been 17 ice ages in the past 100 million years. Each ice age, lasting several million years, is followed by an abrupt warming with glacial retreat and a period of moderate temperatures in the Northern Hemisphere that lasts from 10,000 to 12,000 years. It has been about 11,000 years since the end of the last ice age (so that from a purely statistical basis and assuming that the earth continues these cycles of temperature change, we are indeed due for another ice age!).

We should recall that ice ages are not really a global phenomenon. They are characteristic of the Northern Hemisphere. During ice ages past, great continental ice sheets did not form in South America, Africa, Southeast Asia, or Australia. The temperatures in the tropics remained relatively unchanged.

Moreover, during the current interglacial period, there have been significant climate shifts in the Northern Hemisphere. There are temperature oscillations of about 2,500 years in duration, with warmer periods centered about 1,000, 3,500, and 6,000 years ago and colder periods in between.

Recall the medieval "little optimum" (900 to 1100 A.D.). The Vikings sailed across an iceberg-free North Atlantic Ocean, settled Greenland and probably Labrador, as well. This was followed by the "little ice age" (1430 to 1850). Cold was then so intense that trees froze and exploded from internal ice buildup in Southern England, and the Thames River froze solid at London (1814).

About 6,000 years ago, the Sahara Desert was very different; cave paintings dating from the time show elephants, giraffes, crocodiles, and hippopotamuses. Conclusion: Data do not support temperature rise. Claims based on computer projections cannot be accurate for the next five days. How, then, can we expect them to be accurate in determining weather patterns for the next 50 years!

That brings us to the second disputed situation --- the rise in the atmospheric concentration of CO_2.

So, what do we know about CO_2? Quite a bit, including some little discussed data. And yet, not enough. We know, with considerable certainty, that the CO_2 concentration in the air has increased roughly 25 percent since the beginning of the industrial age --- from 280 parts per million to 365 parts per million (0.035 percent). Is it an easy conclusion, as many people believe, to trace that increase to modern man's burning of fossil fuels? The situation is not so simple. Consider:

- Prehistoric CO_2 levels also changed --- 100 million years ago, there were not 350 parts per million but 3,000 to 5,000 parts per million! This was obviously not due to industry!
- Measuring instruments and techniques for detecting

CO_2 in air and glacial ice have been critically reviewed by Jaworoski and Hisdal of the Norwegian Polar Institute (1990), and they found the range of error to approach 100 percent in the 19th Century carbon-dioxide measurements. They concluded that atmospheric heating by anthropogenic releases of CO_2 have not been proved.

- Estimates show that humans pump about 7 billions tons of CO_2 into the atmosphere every year; in the same period, nature produces about 200 billion tons of CO_2.
- In a remarkable, keenly analyzed paper (1990), Freeman Dyson of the Princeton Institute for Advanced Study examined the sources and sinks for CO_2 and concluded that fully 50 percent could not be accounted for. This corroborates previous conclusions derived by oceanographers. There is clearly much that is still not understood.
- Finally, we should remember that plants love carbon dioxide. A doubling of the CO_2 content under controlled conditions results in a 30 percent increase in growth and yield. It also results in a plant that has stronger, larger leaves and stems, and is more resistant to drought and disease.

From all the above we can only conclude that both the temperature regime and the CO_2 picture deserve greater study and understanding before trillions of dollars are spent to mitigate a problem that may not exist, or, if it does, may not be very important.

Yet the supporters of the global-warming theory are adamant. Here is what Dr. Stephen Schneider of the National Center for Atmospheric Research said:

"We need to get some broad-based support, to capture the public's imagination. That, of course, entails getting loads of media coverage. So we have to offer up scary scenarios, make simplified, dramatic statements, and make little mention of any doubts we may have. Each of us has to decide what is the right balance between being effective and being honest."   ---

(Discovery, October, 1989, p.47).

Now we must tackle the stratospheric ozone layer and its notorious "hole." What do we know for sure about it?

- The ozone layer is not stable; it is in a state of constant turbulence.
- Incoming radiation from the sun --- especially the UV spectrum --- both creates and destroys ozone.
- Variations in the thickness of the ozone layer occur on a seasonal basis and vary according to latitude. Annual fluctuations are up to 25 percent.
- Greater thinning (up to about 50 percent) can occur at the South Pole. Thinning takes place at both poles but is greater in the Antarctic.
- The so-called "hole" or thinning over the Antarctic appears annually at the end of the Antarctic winter; it lasts about 3-to-5 weeks and is then reconstituted. There is no permanent "hole."
- There is no overall loss of ozone.
- Polar thinning is related to the Polar Vortex --- a cyclonic-type storm that forms each year in Antarctica at winter's end.
- Besides extreme cold (-85 degrees C) for several weeks and return of the sunlight (and radiation), ozone "depletion" appears to require the presence of the chloride ion.
- The belief persists that the Cl (chloride) comes from the CFCs (chlorofluorocarbons) --- mainly freons, but there is no documented proof of this, only theory.
- Chloride is one of nature's most abundant ions, with major sources in volcanic eruptions and oceanic storms.

Consider the following:
- The world production of chlorofluorocarbons is 1.1 million tons per year. This accounts for roughly 750,000 tons of chloride.
- Evaporation of sea water provides the atmosphere with 600 million tons of chloride per year.

- Passive outgassing from the earth accounts for 36 million tons of chloride per year.
- Volcanic eruptions emit a few million to hundreds of millions of tons of chloride. Tambora erupted in 1813 with 211 million tons of chloride --- at the present rate of production of CFCs, it would take humans about 282 years to produce as much chloride as this one eruption.
- We are living in a period of greatly increased volcanism; Mount Erebus produces 1,000 tons of chloride daily and has been doing so for 100 years. It is located in Antarctica, 10 kilometers upwind of McMurdo Sound and injects its chlorides directly into the stratosphere.
- Again, how much chloride comes from CFCs? About 0.75 million tons annually. Yet, the amount of chloride calculated to be in the stratosphere at any one time is 50 to 60 times this figure.

If indeed chloride is necessary to the atmospheric breakdown of ozone, whose chloride is it, man's or nature's! There is no documented evidence of CFC molecules in the stratosphere. There are no measurement data, only theory. We can hope that the recently launched instruments to measure the composition of the ozone layer will remedy this.

Recall that the so-called "ozone hole" was discovered in 1956 by the Cambridge meteorologist, Gordon Dobson. It was Dobson who devised the instrumentation and techniques of measuring the stratospheric ozone. He considered the Antarctic ozone thinning to be an anomaly until the phenomenon occurred again in 1957, when he reported it as a natural annual event. The French investigators, P. Rigaue and B. LeRoy, also measured the "hole" in 1958, when it was thinner than at any time since --- and this was in the 1960s, before the widespread use of CFCs. Their conclusion was briefly stated:

"The thinning [is] related to the Polar Vortex ,... and the recovery is sharp and complete." French scientists also related the ozone "depletion" to increased solar activity; "we are now living in a period of greater solar flares and sunspots than at any time since Galileo's day."

Concern about the loss of stratospheric ozone relates to penetration of ultraviolet radiation. The thinner the ozone shield, the greater UV penetration to the earth's surface. But, measuring instruments set up in the U.S. in 1974 showed _no_ increase in surface UV radiation. Moreover, it should not be forgotten that all people, and especially light-skinned ones, require some direct exposure to sunlight (UV) to prevent the development of rickets and/or later onset of osteoporosis or other bone-thinning maladies.

Of course, overexposure to UV radiation can cause skin cancer. This is well established. But people have been unduly frightened by not being told that there are two different kinds of skin cancer. One, related to too much ultraviolet (or sunbathing or tanning salons) is unsightly, irritating, and annoying, but curable in 99 percent of the cases. The other, more rare form is malignant melanoma. This cannot be correlated with exposure to UV, is usually fatal, and appears to be genetically determined. To imply that ozone loss (even if it occurred) would lead to an increase in malignant melanoma is a false and malicious misuse of science.

On April 4, 1991, William Reilly, the administrator of the U.S. Environmental Protection Agency, said:

"...The ozone has thinned 4-5 percent, which doubles the previous estimate. This means 200,000 more cancer deaths over the next 50 years."

He called the situation "grim." His statement was wrong, both as to the purported thinning and the skin cancers. Even if he were right, a 4-to-5 percent increase in exposure to UV is far less than a simple shift to a lower latitude. Moving from Washington, DC to South Florida increases one's UV exposure about 22 percent, and a journey from either pole to the equator subjects a person to a natural increase in UV radiation of 5,000 percent!

Finally, those who would ban the production and use of CFCs on the basis of computer simulations and undocumented theory choose to overlook the reasons chlorofluorocarbons were developed and put into use in the first place. They are non-volatile, non-toxic, and present no direct hazards to living organisms. CFCs are used in refrigeration and air-conditioning equipment, in firefighting (halon foams) and in degreasing and cleaning electronic components. Despite many promises to the contrary, no substitutes have been developed and put into production.

All of the proposed substitutes for CFCs have turned out to be toxic, flammable, corrosive, and inefficient. Use of any of them or a return to cumbersome, ineffective refrigerants, like ammonia or sulfur dioxide, would require total redesign of equipment. In the U.S. alone, there are 5,000 companies that use CFCs; the value of the goods they produce is $28 billion per year.

There are millions of individual and commercial refrigerating and air-conditioning units. The capital investment exceeds $150 million. The entire food transportation and marketing system throughout the Western world depends upon refrigeration. Is it sensible to throw all this away on the flimsy evidence so far offered as a reason to ban CFCs? Why not simply seal the units better and recycle the freeon?

In conclusion, careful scrutiny of the evidence shows that supporting data for both global warming and ozone depletion is sparse and questionable. Yet the U.S. has already entered into an international agreement to ban the production of CFCs --- and the cost of freeon has already gone up 30 percent or more.

Dr. Richard Benedick, who negotiated the CFC ban on behalf of the U.S., has acknowledged that this action sounded the "death knell" for an important part of the chemical industry. Yet he insisted the ban was necessary, even though the scientific basis for it has not been established.

I believe we are entitled to ask "Why?" The costs are enormous, yet they pale by comparison with the financial burden put upon the American people if the "global warming" advocates prevail. The International Conference on Global Climate in Brazil in 1992 called for a further reduction of carbon dioxide, threatening another serious curtailment of American industry and our standard of living. Does our firm knowledge of the problem and its possible consequences justify such a loss and a sacrifice? My answer is a resounding NO!

Remember, too, that our very liberty depends upon a strong and vigorous economy. Destroy that economy and we will also destroy our liberty. In an earlier chapter, I quoted from statements made by Corinthian emissaries to Sparta in the year, 432 B.C., and I must do so again, because it is so clearly applicable today.

"When one is deprived of one's liberty, one is right in blaming not so much the man who puts on the fetters as the one who had the power to prevent him, but did not use it. Why are we still considering whether we have enemies, instead of how we can resist them?"

We still have to fight for what we believe and to sustain the truth.

CHAPTER 7
ENVIRONMENTAL LAW

*A**mong the hundreds of speeches she delivered in her lifetime, this one, made to the University of California's School of Law, was, to me, at least, perhaps the most telling, most humorous, and most effective she ever made. It was delivered just before her death in January, 1994. With slight edits, I reproduce it here.*

***

In my short time here at the university, I have discovered several things of which I was totally ignorant, the most important being that there is an enormous gap between science and law. I have learned in the past day and a half with you that science does not matter in environmental law. It does not count for anything. Most astonishingly, I learned yesterday that potholes in the State of Nebraska are considered to be navigable waters. I am still grappling with that one. First, I want to see the boat!

I want to remind the speaker who made the statement about potholes that there was a court case in the Seventh Circuit about two years ago, which ruled that potholes, drainage ditches, and other isolated bodies of water, including mud puddles not associated with obviously navigable waters, could not be so considered for the purposes of the Clean Water Act.

That information was transmitted to the responsible government agencies. What do you suppose happened? They ignored it and they are still identifying potholes, mud puddles, and what-have-you as navigable waters of the U.S. Well, so be it. We can be flexible in science, but not to the point where we will accept potholes as navigable water.

I would like to comment on the interesting area of environmental law and bring out what seem to me to be some of the pertinent scientific facts that really underlie the issues in the hope that somehow these two great professions, law and science, will come together in the future. I hope that, by the time I finish, some of you might begin to think, maybe just a little bit, that scientific facts have some role to play in environmental law.

With respect to environmental law, I want to comment on the issues from the standpoint of someone totally outside the legal profession --- an interested bystander, if you will, who has been observing the consequences of the application of various laws and regulations, and what this has meant in terms of a number of activities.

Let me start by saying that there is no body of law, I think, that has as absolutely committed, determined, vociferous, and protective a constituency as environmental law does. One wonders a little bit about why that should be so. I believe that one of the answers is that nature has been elevated in the environmental movement to the status of a religion, one that is not human-based.

Indeed, it is a kind of religion that is the ultimate in laissez faire. It holds that everything should be left alone, that nature knows best, that all nature is pure and sacred, and that only man is vile. They would not dare to say "woman," would they?

Well, are they right? What are the consequences of holding to such a philosophy? Curiously enough --- and I may be wrong in this because my experience and my knowledge is not that complete in environmental law --- I believe that there is no environmental law yet passed among the many dozens that defines the term, "environmental law."

It is assumed that everybody knows what the environment is. However, one of the basic problems with environmental laws is that they apply uniformly across the country. The U,S. is blessed with a great variety of natural areas different from one another. A meadow is not a desert, nor a forest, nor a stream, nor a river. We have mountains. We have areas below sea level. We have coasts and various types of shorelines. We have rivers and lakes. We have a tremendous variety of environments. The same problems do not exist in all these areas. And even if they did, the same solutions would not apply.

Let me use ground water as a simple example. If you are concerned about ground water, it makes a big difference whether that ground water is within four feet of the surface, as it is in Florida, or 4,000 feet below the surface, as it is in some of the arid Southwestern states. Science makes a difference in what you are able to do, but the laws apply uniformly with regard to these factors.

We get rules and regulations that indicate how much of this or how much of that shall be considered to be toxic or hazardous without taking hormesis into account.

You all know what "hormesis" is, don't you? The concept of hormesis was first enunciated in the 16th Century by a physician who took the name, Paracelsus. He put it simply:

"There is nothing that is poison and everything is poison."

That is certainly true. It all depends on how much. Thus, when we have rules and laws that tell us that this much of something is poisonous or toxic, it has to have some basis in fact, because the amount for any particular substance will differ.

We have U.S. Environmental Protection Agency (EPA) standards that require, for example, the City of Columbus, Ohio, to hold the amount of atrazine, a herbicide used in some of the surrounding farms and never detected in the city water supply at levels higher than five parts per billion, to only three parts per billion, despite the fact that there is ample scientific evidence showing conclusively that it takes a level of at least 35,000 parts per billion to cause any detectable health effect.

Now, you all know, of course, how much or rather how little a part per billion is. It is not easy to get a mental concept. It is small. It is a tiny bit. It is eenie weenie! To put it simply: One part per billion is equivalent to about one drop of Vermouth in five train-carloads of gin. It is not much.

One of the great failures, if I may use that term, of modern technological society is that instruments have been developed to measure those amounts accurately. They can even measure parts per trillion, and dioxin has to be measured to that amount for the purpose of discharges from pulp mills. One part per trillion would be equivalent to one drop of Vermouth in 5,000 carloads of gin. Is that amount of dioxin dangerous? No. Hazardous? No.

But we have laws that say if you can detect the presence of it at a site, the site is a hazard, it is toxic, and, therefore, it is a Superfund site. Most Superfund sites are identified by such amounts of dioxin. How does the EPA determine whether there is enough toxic material to declare some place a Superfund site? Mostly on the basis of the estimated amount of dioxin present.

They have settled on parts per trillion for dioxin. This standard is based on a risk study which supposes that a child sitting in the midst of such a site eats the dirt 24 hours a day for 70 years and thus would have one chance in a million of contracting cancer. Well, it is conservative.

The question is, "Does it make any sense scientifically?" No. Does it make any sense economically? I would say that the one in a million cutoff adopted by the EPA, the Occupational Safety and Health Administration (OSHA), and other health agencies is based on the induced fear of cancer. That is a risk of one in a million for contracting cancer, not the certainty of the cancer and not a cancer death.

Since 1950, the number of cases of every one of the various kinds of cancer that we know of --- and there are many, many different ones with many different causes --- has been declining, with the exceptions of lung cancer, which is caused by smoking, and certain types of very rare neurological cancers, which could not be identified before present day nuclear medicine.

The fact is that cancer, with the single exception of childhood leukemia, which is really quite rare, is a disease of old age. Because we have such a much expanded life expectancy now, more people are living longer and more people are getting cancer. But when the facts are adjusted for age, every cancer has been declining in amount since 1950. This information seems not to be widely disseminated.

Although most environmental law is based upon the premise that toxic chemicals, the things that are manufactured by human beings, are the cause of most cancers, the fact is that they cause less than one-half of one percent of all of the cancers. That can easily be determined by contact with the National Cancer Institute.

What is it costing the economy in this country to hold to such standards and have environmental regulations and laws set by this means? Well, since it started basing its risk analyses on the possibility of cancer, the EPA has spent more than $6 billion. The entire budget of the National Cancer Institute is $2 billion. There have been several people, including one EPA official, who refuses to be identified publicly, who say the very best thing that the EPA could do to contribute to the understanding and better control of cancer would be to give its entire budget to the National Cancer Institute.

This brings me to another aspect of environmental law. We have too many laws permitting too many agencies to do some of the same things. Let me digress for just a moment to tell you that I come into this area truly from the point of naivete with respect to law. I grew up at a time when we were taught that our nation is a nation of laws. I have always believed that and have had some kind of respect and awe for laws, except the ones I do not happen to obey, like the seatbelt law. We were taught, and I have always understood, that law is made by the legislative branch of government, that law is interpreted and transgressions taken care of by the judicial branch, and that law is administered by the executive branch of government.

In the field of environmental law, that no longer applies for two reasons. The Congress, in its wisdom, has been passing laws either so utterly detailed or so totally ambiguous that it is left up to agencies and the employees of agencies to interpret the laws the way they want. The laws are passed for all the best, good, and noble reasons, but it is left to the agencies to promote regulations that have the force of law.

All of these things give us considerable problems, because we now have to contend with some monster called administrative law, which I do not understand and which seems to have nothing to do with due process or proper rules of evidence.

Nevertheless, all these things have combined to create a situation in which much environmental law and regulation are being imposed and administered by bureaucrats and employees at various levels. A GS-12 can come onto a property and impose a fine on a property owner if he thinks he detects some wetlands or something like that. All these things are being done by one and the same people.

In other words, the bureaucracies are making law, administering law, and punishing transgressions. And, as often has been said, when that happens (and that, to my understanding, was the reason for the separation of powers originally in our government), the power to make the law, to administer it, to interpret it, and to punish transgressions, is concentrated in one branch of government. That constitutes tyranny. I believe that is not too strong a word to describe the way in which environmental law is being applied to the citizens of our great country.

But now let me be a little bit more specific. Let us take water. Incidentally, water is something that cannot be used up. We have as much water today as we ever had or ever will have. We cannot make water. I mean that in the purely scientific sense, of course. We cannot produce it. We can only use it and it recirculates. Generally, it recirculates in a large system that carries water into the oceans, from which the water evaporates into clouds and returns all over the Earth, including the land, as rain. It is always the same amount.

What we really have to be thinking about with respect to water is the way in which we use it. If we put it this way, can anybody believe that it makes good sense to go to all the trouble to make sure that the water is totally safe and clean for drinking and cooking purpose, and then use it to wash our cars, to flush our toilets, to water the garden, or to use for industrial processes? No. We demand potable water for everything, and that is where our problems lie. *What we should be thinking about is developing dual systems so that we retain potable watger for personal uses only. I think that this may come some day.*

Now, in the 1977 Clean Water Act, there are extensive definitions that refer to the purpose of restoring and maintaining the integrity of the nation's waters. What better purpose could we have? Restore and maintain the integrity of the nation's waters. Restore to what level? What is the original integrity of the waters and how does that get maintained?

If one then looks at the definition that is applied to polluted water, and what constitutes pollution of water, we find that in the end nothing except distilled water can legally be discharged into any natural body or onto the land. It would be better if that water was triply distilled, because, under the Clean Water Act, this is how pollution of the water is defined: "The term, 'pollutant,' means dredged spoil, solid waste, incinerator residues, sewage, garbage, sewage sludge, munitions, chemical wastes, biological materials, radioactive materials, heat, wrecked or discarded equipment, rock, sand, cellar dirt and industrial, municipal, and agricultural waste discharged into water."

None of these can be discharged legally in any amount into our natural waters. So one has to ask the question: "What is not a pollutant?" Distilled water. Does it make any sense? Scientifically, no. But, from what I have learned from you guardians of the law in the past couple days, maybe legally, yes!

When the first Clean Water Act was passed in 1972, it covered requirements for the analysis of about two dozen different pollutants. I just read to you the list of general categories of pollutants that must now be analyzed for any certified municipal potable water supply. And if we break down these categories, the list actually amounts to more than 300 identified hazardous or toxic materials, even though in any one system only about four or five of them would be important. Nevertheless, every single drinking water system is required to analyze for all 300. You all wonder why your water bills are going up?

Under the latest amendments, lead and chlorine content are also tested. We now have, by tenfold, the most rigid requirement in the world for lead content, and there is no good scientific basis for it at all. When this amendment was being considered, even Congressman Dingell pointed out that the studies on which the EPA based its lead standard were false and that the people involved had, and I quote Mr. Dingell, "cooked the books." Nevertheless, that is the standard that we have. It is costing an enormous amount of money. Now, there's real waste for you!

The second standard is chlorine. The greatest contribution to public health that was ever made, as far as water is concerned, was the introduction of water chlorination. That is the primary reason we have conquered practically all waterborne diseases in the U.S. But in its wisdom, the EPA recognized that chlorine has byproducts, such as chloroform, which is produced if you heat the water. There was an internal paper produced questioning whether small amounts of chloroform from the chlorination of water supplies might lead to an infinitesimal number of cancer risks.

So far, nobody in this country has taken that paper seriously. But not too long ago, it was taken seriously in Chile.

The Chileans stopped chlorinating the water supplies in their cities. Just at the same time a shipload of contaminated seafood arrived in port and started a cholera epidemic, which continued for some time throughout South America --- all because they believed, on the basis of an EPA report from the U.S., that chlorination might possibly cause some cancer.

A second paper circulated, also from the EPA, which pointed out that, if you breathe the steam produced by heating chlorinated water, you have to breathe some chloroform, and chloroform at some level can be shown to be carcinogenic. But, remember, everything is poison and nothing is poison. The EPA has not determined at what level it is carcinogenic, but the agency has proposed a new rule that makes taking showers with chlorinated water illegal, because you breathe the steam in an enclosed area, thereby putting yourself at some risk. Your health is going to be protected whether you want it to be or not.

Cancer from water pollution has never been reported to have occurred; yet we are controlling many, many such pollutants, even though we have already removed from natural waters and from the ambient atmosphere, about 90 percent of all the identified pollutants that were there about 20 years ago.

One of the things that is seldom mentioned is how much credit we should be given for improving things over the past three or four decades. Of course, the environmental laws have helped. But like so many good things, they can go overboard and we are now getting, I think, into the area of no return.

According to statements from the EPA, in cleaning up 90 percent of the known air and water pollutants, we have made tremendous improvements in air and water quality, but it has cost us a lot of money. Ninety percent cleanup has, so far, cost $1.4 trillion dollars. There are those who say 90 percent is not good enough and that we have to clean up some more. Let's make it 95 percent. Calculations from the EPA hold that for cleaning up the next 5 percent, it will cost an additional $1.6 trillion!

The time has come to ask the question: "How clean is

clean enough?" How much can we afford to spend? How much can we burden our economy with costs that cannot be shown to have any measurable impact on a problem that might not be real? If we look back over the things that we have done besides the cleanups, we have made some mistakes. We have considered some things to be hazardous and have gone to a lot of expense and effort to clean them up, only to find that they were not a problem at all.

Do you remember the cranberry scare? It turned out to be nothing. Do you remember red dye No. 2? And saccharine? And cyclamates? Do you remember the mercury in tuna and in swordfish? It turned out that there was less mercury in their flesh than was dissolved in the waters of the oceans.

Do you remember the evacuation of Times Beach, Missouri, on the basis of infinitesimal amounts of dioxin contained in the used oil that was spread to keep down the dust of the dirt streets? After nearly ten years of study on dioxin at the Centers for Disease Control and Prevention in Atlanta, Georgia, Dr. Vernon Houk, who ordered the evacuation of Times Beach at a cost of about $140 million to taxpayers to relocate everybody in that small town, found that the amount of dioxin present in Times Beach exposed the people there to a risk no greater than drinking two beers in a lifetime. Times Beach is still vacant!

Then we have PCBs. The worst thing that has ever happened to people exposed to massive amounts of PCBs is the development of a skin irritation called chloracne. Nothing else. And there have been massive contaminations. But because there was a theory that it might cause cancer somehow, PCBs were banned from use in electrical transformers. It was the only material we ever had that was not flammable and could operate in these systems. As a result of the ban, there have been a number of electrical fires in city systems across the country. More people have been burned and killed from these fires because of the loss of the PCBs than ever would have been hurt by their use.

Now, a substance that has just been included in the list of

toxic and hazardous materials under the EPA's control is quartz --- a proper mineral term for sand. Sand is now considered a hazardous material! If you buy sand for a sandbox for a youngster, the package has to say: "Danger, this material is carcinogenic." Yes, beach sand.

Moreover, the minerals that are now coming under control under the same toxic and hazardous rubric include iron, chromium, and selenium. I mentioned these three because they have been eliminated entirely from water under the Safe Drinking Water Act. Iron is absolutely essential in our diet or we get anemia, but not too much iron. Enough, but not too much. If we lack chromium, which we usually get from the water, we are subject to diabetes. It is essential. Selenium is essential to prevent heart disease.

What are we doing to ourselves by taking an absolutist sort of attitude against these materials? As I look at it, I think we have trouble with environmental law on three levels. First, there are those actions taken by bureaucracies in promulgating regulations and in enforcing them that are not based either on common sense or on good science. If we look at wetlands for just a moment, the wetlands, of course, do not have a statute. There is no law that either identifies or says that wetlands have to be protected, none at all. The protection of wetlands comes under Section 404 of the Clean Water Act, which gives control to the Corps of Engineers over the dumping of drilling materials and sludge into the navigable waters of the U.S.

Now, in trying to define what the term "wetlands" means, since it is not defined in law, the White House set up a group of agencies with some interest in wetlands. Not only the Corps of Engineers, but the EPA, the Fish and Wildlife Service, and the Soil Conservation Service have defined "wetland." They did so in 1987 and modified the definition in 1988. The trouble is that the definition has 50 different interpretations. You can take your pick.

The one that is most widely used defines wetlands as any soil, any piece of ground, where water can be shown to rise within 18 inches of the surface for five consecutive days during the year. As a result of that definition, 40 percent of California is wetlands. There are a lot of wetlands in the desert. More than 90 percent of Alaska is wetlands. All of the Midwest is wetlands, and so is Washington, DC.

I started reading a list of things that we had been afraid of and then found that, after some expense, they turned out not to be important at all. Two of these are really serious. One is asbestos and the other is acid rain.

Let's take acid rain first. In 1980, Congress authorized a study and allocated $500 million to get the best experts in the country working on the National Acid Precipitation Assessment Program. There were more than 500 scientists working on it, and they were the best experts in the many different areas related to acid rain and its effect on forests, lakes, stream, rivers, and so on.

The upshot of the ten-year study, which cost taxpayers about $540 million, was that they were able to show in 47 volumes worth of evidence that the impact of acid rain on the Eastern U.S., particularly New England, was indeed a nuisance, but no catastrophe, no big problem. No serious or deleterious impact on any of the forests, except the Red Spruce in the high Adirondacks, which had been a stressed forest even in the preceding century, was shown.

The scientists were able to show without question that less than one percent of all the lakes, rivers, and streams had been acidified. The problem in New England was that the soil itself was a poor, granitic soil. It has always been acidic and always will be. For a short period of time, when deforestation was taking place, the ash from the burning sludge and the residue from the trees that were cut down made the soil alkaline, and that changed the pH of the lakes. As soon as that was all gone and the place reverted to farmland, towns, countryside, and so on, it became acidic again, just as it had always been.

If one wanted to get rid of the acidity of the lakes, the one percent of them that have been affected by industrial affluence from the Ohio Valley, it could be done by using lime at a cost of about $50 million. Indeed, when the report was completed, those who were in charge of it were asked how much benefit could be gained by the controls and the treatments, and things like that, and the answer was $100 million worth of benefit probably for a cost of many times more than that.

But more importantly, and what has not been widely released, is that we found that the acid rain has positive benefits. That has to do with New England. New England is very heavily forested now. It has happened almost without people realizing it. There was a time when New England was clear-cut and there were farms and small villages everywhere. It has largely gone back to a forested area.

In fact, the State of Maine is more heavily forested than any other state in the nation. Ninety percent of the territory of Maine is covered by forests. Indeed, the forests of New England are some of the most vigorously growing and healthy forests in the country. Why? Because of acid rain. Because the sulfates and the nitrates, which are essential for plant growth, were carried by the polluted atmosphere blowing up from the industrialized Ohio Valley to the New England soil, which lacked sulfates and nitrates.

Of course, that is not what was supposed to happen. Incidentally, that information is also available in Sweden and in other parts of Scandinavia, which have discovered the same thing. When you have a soil that lacks these nutrients, this material can be supplied by so-called acid rain. It is, in fact, called the poor farmer's fertilizer. How much money should we spend removing those materials, those valuable materials? If we do that, you know, the forests are affected again, because they are not getting their proper nutrients.

I would like to pick up again on the three levels I spoke of, the actions taken by bureaucrats under laws that do not specify how far they can go. The second level is that laws are passed which explicitly or implicitly require certain actions as, for example, through regulations that count as laws affecting wetlands.

Just to make a quick observation in the first place, nobody knows how much U.S. territory was swamp, marsh, or bog when the pilgrims landed, because nobody was doing geological surveys at that time. So it is only a guess how much marsh land and swamps we have ever had. But we are going to return it all to that original state, whatever it was.

In any case, we are protecting areas that are wet, as well as areas that qualify under definition. In doing so, we are inadvertently also protecting the mosquitoes. As a result, we are having outbursts of hordes of mosquitoes in many parts of the U.S. at the present time to the extent that people in Florida and the Upper Middle West, probably into New Jersey, cannot leave their homes after the sun goes down because the mosquitoes are so numerous.

We cannot control the mosquitoes, of course, because you cannot use pesticides on wetlands. Heaven help us! We cannot pour oil on those waters, and we cannot drain them! So the mosquitoes are proliferating. That would be only a nuisance were it not for the fact that the mosquitoes have a bad habit of biting people; they are blood suckers. I know of no redeeming quality possessed by mosquitoes.

However, when they bite us, besides taking our blood, they can and often do insert parasites. Some of the worst diseases known to the human race, scourges of the centuries, have been carried by mosquitoes. We get those diseases only by being bitten by a mosquito. They include malaria and encephalitis, two of the worst diseases that we know about, because once you contract them, you cannot be cured. The symptoms can be treated and the pain can be relieved. But once you get malaria, you have it forever. Once you get encephalitis, the same thing is true.

Encephalitis is a particularly vicious disease because it is a virus carried by the mosquito, and once in the bloodstream, it never leaves the body. Sometimes, even years after the first episode, one may get a simple cold or a sore throat and so on, and then it breaks out again with enormous brain damage. That is the end result of most cases of encephalitis.

We used to have epidemics of encephalitis. We are having them again. We used to have parts of our country almost unlivable because of malaria. We have had a tenfold increase in the number of cases of malaria in this country since we started protecting wetlands.

Sooner or later, my friends, we are going to have to sit down and make a decision. Either we continue to protect wetlands and protect mosquitoes or we are going to protect human health. We are going to have to choose which is more important. Worse than that, I suspect it will be made more difficult because, in the intervening few years, we have had a lot of immigration into this country from parts of the world bringing in new types of mosquitoes and new types of mosquito parasites that are going to cause outbreaks of such things as Dengue fever, bone break fever, yellow fever, and so on.

There is not time to continue giving you all these sorts of examples, but I want to mention the third phase of law, the development of international environmental treaties, and I have to tell you very bluntly, none of them is based on supportable and verifiable science.

The first one is the Climate Change Treaty, to address the so-called global warming. There is no evidence whatsoever to support the widely held belief that the earth is warming up. All of the evidence points the other way. Before long, I think we are going to see enough new information made public, even if we have to hammer down the doors of the newspapers and television studios to do it, to show that the whole global-warming thing is nothing more than normal variation, and that there is no reason to believe that producing carbon dioxide is causing any kind of climate change whatsoever.

That will soon be followed, although it will take a little longer time, by the questions with respect to ozone. As with global warming, everything that supports the notion that CFCs or other things are destroying the ozone layer in our stratosphere is based upon theory and computer models. There is no direct evidence. The measurements that have been taken find CFC molecules barely reaching the lower stratosphere and then in amounts of only one or two parts per trillion. That is nowhere near enough to be able to do anything to the ozone layer at all.

Moreover, in all the stories about the ozone, what is totally overlooked are those places --- for example, a meteorological station in Belgium --- where ozone measurements have been taken continuously 24 hours a day on a daily basis since 1971. They show natural variations in the amount of ozone of as much as 40 percent from day to day. There is much more evidence for other parts of the world. We have been misled because information the public needs has not been widely disseminated.

Indeed, when it comes to these international treaties, I have to ask this question: "Who negotiates them?" I ask that from the perspective of a very brief period in my checkered past, when, for five months, I was an Assistant Secretary in the Department of State. I believed then and I still want to believe now that international treaties are negotiated through the Secretary of State.

Did the Secretary of State go to Rio de Janeiro, along with President Bush when he was forced by public opinion to sign the Climate Change Treaty? No, he never saw it. Did he have anything to do with the Montreal Protocol? No. That was negotiated by a functionary within the Department of State by the name of Richard Benedick, who was careless enough to write a book about it. It is called Ozone Diplomacy. In it he says that the signatory countries sounded the death knell for an important part of the chemical industry with implications for billions of dollars in investment and hundreds of thousands of jobs in related sectors.

Perhaps the most extraordinary aspect of the treaty was its imposition of short-term economic costs to protect human health and the environment against unproved future human dangers, dangers that rested on scientific theory rather than on firm data. At the time of negotiation and signing, no measurable evidence of damage existed. None does today.

But we have these nice theories, and so I want to call your attention in closing to something said by a very wise man a very long time ago. The year was 1530. And the man's name was Nicolo Machiavelli. He said that a hypothesis is always more believable than a truth, for a theory can be tailored to our thinking and our already established beliefs --- whereas the truth is only its own clumsy self. Ergo, never seek the truth when a hypothesis will do.

CHAPTER 8
ANOTHER OUTRAGEOUS EPA BAN

This message, written by Dr. Ray just a few months before she died, represents one of her most important criticisms of the EPA and the environmental extremists. She could not understand why this outrageous ban, so costly to all farmers and to the nation, has not been reported by the news media nor by all the farmers' associations in America.

***

Just 24 hours before he left office, former Administrator of the EPA, William K. Reilly, gave the American people a parting "gift." He banned methyl bromide. This unilateral action will result in huge increases in the cost of food and a reduction in the amount, quality, and safety of our food supply.

The announcement, made in a January 19, 1993 press release, provided for a series of actions, including:

1. A ban on all halons, effective January 1, 1994. That allowed for only one year to phase out the most important and effective fire suppressant available. No substitute has been developed. I have dealt with this ban in an earlier chapter.

2. A ban on all CFCs, carbon tetrachloride, and methyl chloroform had been expected, but he also included HBFCs, which came as a surprise, since there has been no research to substantiate the action. The ban on these substances was made effective January 1, 1996.
3. The ban on methyl bromide was to begin with a freeze; controls and limited use would start by January 1, 1994, followed by total elimination on January 1, 2000.

It is worth noting that Mr. Reilly took the action, which would seriously burden the domestic economy, even though a similar effort failed to get international support of the parties to the 1987 Montreal Protocol at its November, 1992 meeting in Copenhagen. The nations that signed the ozone treaty met to consider amendments and changes, including a proposal from the U.S. to add methyl bromide to the list of banned substances. That effort failed, even though it was pushed hard by the EPA, which was backed by the NRDC, Friends of the Earth, and other activist environmental organizations.

Many of the Third World nations objected strongly to losing methyl bromide, as did France, Italy, Spain, Greece, and Israel. Among the African nations, Kenya fought the ban most fiercely. And so, losing internationally, the EPA apparently believed that unilateral action by the U.S. could force the issue.

In an accompanying statement that supported the proposal, Reilly said:

"The accelerated phaseout is the centerpiece of EPA's overall program to eliminate the substances most responsible for destroying our stratospheric ozone layer. It will help restore ozone to its normal levels by the middle of the next century, thus preventing millions of cases of skin cancer and cataracts."

Although Reilly once again called up the twin specters of skin cancer and cataracts (more on this important subject later), the immediate justification for doing away with methyl bromide was the belief that it destroys stratospheric ozone. But is this really true? No evidence supports it. Since the economic consequences of the ban are so severe, it is imperative that proof of harm be demonstrated. That has not been done.

In proposing the ban, the EPA was clearly acting within its authority, because the 1990 Clean Air Act Amendments require the agency to eliminate ozone depleters. Despite this Congressional mandate, there is much disagreement and a great deal of scientific uncertainty as to whether stratospheric ozone is being depleted at all. And, even if it should be, there is no direct evidence --- no data --- that halogen-containing compounds are responsible.

The hypothesis rests wholly on computer models and simulations, not in measurements and facts. But from a practical, political viewpoint, the question is moot; by international treaty, the U.S. is obliged to remove from use all CFCs and related compounds. Reilly's proposal, already submitted to the Federal Register, added methyl bromide to this company of outlawed, man-made chemicals.

Should this be a cause of concern? Most assuredly, yes! The loss of CFCs impacts all refrigeration, domestic and commercial, and all air conditioning, as I have already indicated. And the cost worldwide for less efficient substitutes and required new equipment is estimated at $5 trillion! How much more can the American economy absorb?

For an answer to that question, we must first examine just what methyl bromide is and how it is used. Methyl bromide is a fairly simple molecule with one atom of carbon, three of hydrogen (a "methyl" group), and one atom of bromine. In the words of George Dunlop, president of the United Fresh Fruit and Vegetable Association, it is used "virtually ubiquitously as a benign and irreplaceable fumigant and fungicide."

Methyl bromide is versatile and effective. It is used both domestically and internationally in the production of more than 100 different crops. These include a wide range of vegetables and fruits, as well as flowers, ornamental plants, and turf. It was first introduced in 1930, and the variety of uses kept growing thereafter.

It is indispensable to fumigate soils before planting.

Injected into the ground as a liquid, methyl bromide is quickly volatilized and penetrates even into the smallest pores in the soil before evaporating harmlessly into the air. It kills such abundant and harmful pests as nematodes, insect larvae, and toxic fungi. It does NOT contaminate ground water or leave any residue on produce. By eliminating pests in the soil, use of methyl bromide as a fumigant leads to stronger root systems for the plants, greater resistance to drought and disease, and an increase in crop yields of as much as 500 percent.

Methyl bromide is used to sterilize both storage and transportation facilities, and to protect cereal grains and other agricultural commodities that are shipped some distance to market or require long-term storage. Foods that move in international trade require the protection from infection that methyl bromide provides.

In the U.S. virtually all imported fruits and vegetables are fumigated at the port of entry; this is required by law. Methyl-bromide treatment protects against the introduction of devastating pests --- not only microorganisms and insects but also such creatures as the giant Italian land snail. Similar requirements in other countries require fumigation by methyl bromide to prevent the introduction of American pests --- for example, wheat rust, Hessian flies on or in sweet cherries, etc.

Of course, there are some alternatives to methyl bromide. For disinfesting and disinfecting foodstuffs, the use of gamma radiation comes to mind. But it takes years to build and license a food irradiation plant (only one was operating in the U.S. at the time), and the opponents of pesticides like methyl bromide (NRDC and others) hate food irradiation even more --- for even less cause.

Another important use for methyl bromide is as a fumigant for homes and other buildings that have been invaded by termites, carpenter ants, or other vermin (cockroaches, mice, etc.) in food-processing facilities. Presently, there is no alternative as safe and simple to handle --- and as effective.

Finally, methyl bromide is valuable as
- An effective herbicide against several noxious weeds.

- A solvent in dye manufacture.
- A dry-cleaning agent for de-greasing wool.
- An important fire-fighting chemical.
- An intermediary chemical in the manufacture of important pharmaceuticals.

Why should so useful and versatile a chemical be banned? No claim of harm to human health has been made, and methyl bromide hasn't even been accused of being a carcinogen. Indeed, one of its positive attributes is that it stinks to high heaven in extremely low concentrations. It is thus easily detectable in amounts far, far below any that could be harmful. In this respect, it is much safer than carbon dioxide (also used as a fire retardant and preferred by some "environmentalists") since CO_2 cannot be detected by odor and has therefore caused deaths by asphyxiation.

With methyl bromide banned, other pesticides that are not nearly so benign have to be used to avoid large crop losses. Neither this nor any of the economic consequences of removing methyl bromide --- consequences like increased rot and decay of food --- have been taken into account in the Reilly proposal. Estimaters put these costs at about 46.7 billion dollars per year for American consumers. Additionally, many farmers would be ruined. How many can we afford to lose? All for what? A supposed diminution in the amount of stratospheric ozone? Who says so? On what basis?

Reilly asserted that the EPA has determined the "ozone depletion potential" of methyl bromide is 0.7. The law (Clean Air Act Amendments, 1990) requires immediate banning of any substance with an "ozone depletion potential" of 0.2 or more; that puts methyl bromide in jeopardy. But how was this 0.7 potential determined? As usual, the EPA didn't say. No information was provided on just what research was performed, if any, and what the results were. Simply saying, as the EPA does, that the "evidence is compelling" means nothing. Saying doesn't make it so.

A number of scientists employed at NASA, NOAA, and the UN Environmental Program keep repeating that mantra when what we need are accurate data. And a few individuals admit that there are some uncertainties. Not the least of the doubts come from the fact that between 75 percent and 95 percent of all the methyl bromide in the atmosphere comes from natural sources --- not produced by human activity.

Methyl bromide is found in measurable quantities throughout the Earth's atmosphere. It is especially prevalent over shore land and shallow seas. Its source is the ocean, NOT industrial society. Most methyl bromide is produced by living organisms as part of a widely utilized process call methylation.

Many creatures, especially microorganisms, the larger sea weeds, and marine invertebrates, are capable of detoxifying a large number of otherwise hazardous substances. They do this by the process of methylation whereby the methyl group (CH_3) is added to the offending material. The result is that methylated compounds are soluble and also volatile and can evaporate harmlessly, thus eliminating them from the plant or animal's body.

Methylation also occurs in some bogs and swamps, and on land in vegetation like the succulent ice plant which thrives above the high tide along shores swept by salt-laden oceanic winds. These processes put methyl bromide into the atmosphere. According to research reported by atmospheric scientist Hanwent Singh, published in the Journal of Geophysical Research, April 20, 1983, "....this source is large enough to account for virtually the entire tropospheric burden of these (methylated) compounds."

Singh calculated that the ocean produces more than 300,000 tons of methyl bromide annually. Later work by Wuosmaa and Hager, published in <u>Science</u> (July 13, 1990) reported discovery of the enzyme responsible for the synthesis of methyl halides by both marine and terrestrial organisms.

Even the environmentalists' own Guru, James E. Lovelock, reported in his 1979 book, <u>Gaia: A New Look at Life on Earth</u>, that methylation is a common phenomenon in marine life. What is not so well remembered is that Lovelock also reported on his finding of "halo carbons" in nature. He writes, on Page 104:

"Wherever we sailed, we found it easy to detect and measure the fluorochlorocarbon gases, and this discovery lead directly to the present, possibly exaggerated concern over their capacity to deplete the ozone layer."

Well! So much for the activist ozone depletion supporters' claim that CFCs do not occur naturally. They would have us believe that there is no natural sink for CFCs --- or for methyl bromide. Supposedly they float around in the atmosphere forever unless disintegrated by ultraviolet light and broken down through natural processes.

With methyl bromide, current theory holds that once in the atmosphere, the bromine atoms are released to combine with other oxygen or hydrogen. For some unexplained reason, NASA scientists claim that the oxygenated compound destroys the stratospheric ozone and that the hydrogenated compound does not. But independent measurements have established that the bromine hydrogen molecule exists in far greater quantities than predicted from the models. In any event, the stratospheric chemistry on which the "ozone depletion potential" depends has a 10-fold degree of uncertainty! (100%).

Question: Should a policy decision with such far-reaching and costly consequences as that of banning methyl bromide be based on so uncertain and flimsy a foundation of unverified scientific "facts"?

Moreover, as is typical for many things --- from radiation to poisonous, toxic substances and carcinogens that are and always have been part of the Earth's normal environment --- those that occur naturally are ignored by the zealous activists. If the material is "natural," it is OK; if it is man-made, it is evil and causes catastrophes. That this is pure nonsense doesn't seem to matter. If anything is manufactured by humans and used to improve the lot of mankind, it is ruthlessly attacked. So it is with methyl bromide and anything else that is claimed to interact with stratospheric ozone.

The role of methyl bromide as an "ozone depleter" should be evaluated in the context of the entire ozone-layer-destruction theory. This is based on a computer simulation, not on a body of measured evidence. Consider the following:

- The ozone concentration in the stratosphere at 20-40 kilometers above the Earth's surface is about 6 molecules of ozone per million molecules of air. This is hardly a "layer." But it is a higher concentration than in the troposphere.
- Ozone is constantly being produced in the stratosphere by the action of ultraviolet radiation on oxygen molecules. Several tons of ozone (O_3) are produced per minute ($O_2+UV=O=O$) $+O_2=O_3$) whenever the sun is above the horizon.
- The ozone molecule is relatively unstable; it can break down to produce oxygen. It also interacts with other materials in the stratosphere --- chloride, nitrate, aerosols --- to form other compounds.
- The amount of ozone that can be measured at any particular time, at any one place, is the result of the formation and/or breakdown process.
- Variations in the amount of ozone occur naturally on a seasonal basis and according to latitude.
- On a longer scale, variations in the amount of ozone occur according to changes in the sun's radiance with the +/-11 year sun-spot cycle.
- Ozone amounts increase and decrease and increase again on a years-long cycle.
- The smallest amount of stratospheric ozone was measured in the year 1958.
- There is no "normal" amount of ozone.
- If the amount of ozone decreases by 50 percent or more, this is, by agreement, called a "hole."
- The famous Antarctic (seasonal) ozone "hole" was described by Dr. Reginald Dobson during International Geophysical Year 1956-57, before CFCS were in widespread use.
- Norwegian data taken at the observatory in Tromso

record small ozone "holes" dating from the 1930s, long before CFCs were manufactured.
- All variations in ozone amounts are temporary --- that includes the so-called "hole."
- There is no overall loss or trend toward permanent loss of stratospheric ozone.
- For as long as the sun shines and sends out UV radiation, and for as long as there is oxygen in the Earth's atmosphere, there will be ozone produced in the stratosphere.

That leaves the question of human health still to be addressed. If ozone in the stratosphere is being destroyed, there would be more UV reaching the Earth's surface. To date, all the measurements show that is not the case. A network of UV measuring stations, set up across the U.S. and operating from 1974 to 1984 showed NO increase in UV penetration.

The health connection comes from the well established relationship between exposure to UV and skin cancer --- in white people. Common skin cancers, squanous, and basal cell are carcinomas and are almost exclusively confined to light-skinned individuals. Such cancers have been increasing for several decades; so, also, has exposure been increasing through sunbathing, scanty outdoor clothing, tanning parlors, etc. These skin cancers are unpleasant but seldom fatal. They can be cured in 99 percent of the cases.

I realize I have made these comments in an earlier chapter, but they're worth repeating to prove the point. Malignant melanoma, on the other hand, is most often fatal, but, despite many people's belief to the contrary, has not been linked to exposure to sunlight. Not only does it generally appear on parts of the body unlikely to receive extensive exposure (buttocks, soles of the feet, armpits, scalp under the hairline); it is also much more common among office workers than those who spend long hours outside. And it affects dark-skinned as well as light-skinned individuals.

Much emphasis is put on the possible, frightful development of skin cancer as a result of UV exposure. Few people recall that most mammals, certainly including humans, must absorb some UV radiation in order to achieve normal, healthy skeletal growth. Too little UV exposure can lead to a dreadful childhood disease --- rickets --- which was once common in the Northern European countries.

Too little UV exposure can also lead to the onset of osteomalcia --- brittle, easily broken bones in the elderly. While there are roughly 300,000 cases of skin cancer annually in the U.S., there are about one-and-a-half million bone fractures generally of the femur or hip which cause enormous pain and hardship for older people.

And finally there are the widely publicized cases of ozone UV hysteria in New Zealand and Patagonia. Blind sheep and rabbits in Patagonia and Southern New Zealand were claimed to be victims of cataracts caused by increased UV penetration through the Antarctic ozone "hole" --- that is, until an enterprising reporter from KGO-TV in San Francisco traveled to Patagonia to see for himself. He found sheep, true, and was able to obtain eye specimens for post-mortem examination.

It turned out, as reported by medical personnel at the University of California Veterinary College in Davis, California, that the animals, both domestic and wild, suffered from a virulent epidemic of "pink eye," which, in the absence of medical treatment, blinded them.

Finally, we should not leave the subject of methyl bromide and the ozone layer without recounting the story of the Bromine Bomb.

In 1975, Mike McElroy of Harvard University announced that bromine was so effective at destroying the "ozone layer" that it could become a lethal weapon if employed over enemy territory! According to the Harvard scientist, if bromine were injected into the stratosphere above the enemy's home area, it would eat a huge hole in the stratospheric ozone layer and allow penetration of UV radiation to incapacitate the enemy troops and civilians and destroy crops. "A few kilograms of bromine," he said, "is all that would be needed for a large, devastating effect."

McElroy received considerable coverage for his Bromine Bomb --- from the National Enquirer, a fitting publication for such pseudo science. Even so, it was McElroy's "Doomsday Weapon" theory that formed the original basis for the present banning of methyl bromide and the brominated chlorocarbons or halons --- the finest fire extinguishers ever developed.

Science is not free from fads and hysteria; nor do all scientists maintain an objective devotion to provable evidence. But to base public policy on questionable science and to permit enormous expenditures of public funds and widespread hardship for unproven hypotheses is totally unsupportable.

CHAPTER 9
OVERDUE: A SUPREME COURT OF SCIENCE

*T*hroughout the greater part of her career, Dr. Ray expressed a devout wish for the creation of her brainchild, A Supreme Court of Science. She shared the idea with a few other scientists, including a Massachusetts physicist, Dr. Arthur Kantrowitz. I mentioned it in my biography of Dr. Ray, *Is It True What They Say About Dixy?*, way back in 1980 --- but it still remains a dream, unrecognized by Congress. It certainly bears repeating and detailing.

***

How dangerous are pesticides? Can they be used under certain controlled conditions? Is the danger exaggerated or under-rated?

Is timberland clear-cutting ruinous, as some environmentalists insist, or beneficial to tree growth and the land, as some forestry experts contend? Is it ruinous in one place but a blessing in another?

What are the facts and what are the fairy tales in the controversy over constructing more nuclear plants in the energy crisis? How can we separate the emotional responses from the clear truth?

How is a free, democratic nation to make the increasing number of scientifically oriented decisions of the future?

The elitists might say, leave it to the scientists, the technologists, and the engineers to make the big decisions. As a scientist, I say they must never be given that final authority; it must always be the public's right.

But, the elitists might declaim with much justification that the public is not qualified, nor willing, nor interested in making the complicated decisions.

And I must answer that public officials and scientists themselves are to blame for the public's indifference. They have always retained the ultimate power for decision-making themselves and have not acknowledged the public's role.

It would be ludicrous to assume that all persons, then, must be forced to become experts in all the sciences. The scientists themselves are experts only in one or two fields. How, then, is the public to be equipped so it can assist in the final decision-making?

A long-range view would be to revolutionize America's science education. We do an excellent job of training those who go into science and technology, but we turn our scientific noses up at those who don't.

Why don't we teach science appreciation, just as we offer music, art, history, math, and language instruction to those who will not become musicians, artists, historians, mathematicians, and linguists?

The few science courses we do provide leave much to be desired. What do students remember? Why, they may recall cutting up a frog. They don't know where their stomachs are or what the digestive system is supposed to do, but they remember the gore and the excitement of the frog's demise, and not much else.

But so much for the long-range requirement. We cannot wait, because many decisions will have to be made while we're recasting our education system.

First, we must have greater scientific and technological help at the very top. A science adviser or advisory panel should be appointed and assigned to the White House, available to the President constantly. He should not have to rely on political sources alone for scientific wisdom.

How is the President --- who is the world's busiest executive --- to measure crises, legislation, and conflicts that derive directly from highly sophisticated scientific or technological issues? He must have good advice, and sometimes instantly.

But that advice must, of necessity, be confidential, for the President's ears alone.

The Congress and the public need advice and counsel of their own, and such information must be transmitted openly and quickly, except in matters that must be kept secret to maintain national security.

Why Congress? Doesn't it have access to the nation's finest brainpower, and doesn't each senator and representative have a staff?

Yes, but congressmen have a thousand things to do. They cannot devote much time to personal research, except in a crisis condition.

And their staffs? I can say unequivocally that one of the grave dangers in congressional decision-making lies with the personnel some congressmen employ as "experts." The lawmakers cannot afford to hire scientists --- and they should not do so if they could.

One senator has a staff assistant who is so pollution-conscious that he keeps finding smog under every bed. He so advises the senator, and that otherwise bright gentleman has been brainwashed against virtually all forms of scientific and technological progress.

What that senator and all other congressmen --- and the public --- need desperately is something like a "Supreme Court of Science" to help in the decision-making process.

A court of science, appointed by the President with the consent of the Senate, would make no decisions itself and no rulings. It would simply call for arguments on all sides of an issue, provide adversary machinery to get out the facts, run the "trial" by applying all the rules of evidence, then issue a report of findings. But it would not offer an opinion or a decision.

In that way, the Naders, Kendalls, Taylors, Commoners, and their adherents would be given equal time, along with those who champion new processes, developments, and ideas in science and technology. Those who would make wild statements they could not justify with reasonable findings would be ruled out of order and their "evidence" laid aside.

It's an excellent way for Congress and the public to find out who the legitimate debaters are. It's a perfect way to lay aside the emotional arguments and the hysteria and underscore the real facts, the truth.

More important, it would give Congress and the public a chance to do something they haven't been able to do in recent years because of the hysteria: Weigh the evidence and decide which risk they prefer.

It should be obvious to everyone that the big decisions of the future will involve risks. But it is, in the end, the public that must make the final decisions in a nation that intends to remain strong and free.

CHAPTER 10
THE MOUSE IS STILL ROARING

*T*he satirical depiction of a relatively small underdeveloped nation as "The Mouse That Roared" was not lost on Dr. Ray, although she professed great concern for the have-not countries. However, her patience was often exhausted by the abuse heaped upon the U.S. for not doing enough for those nations.

***

The Mouse that roared is not only still roaring. It is trying to drown out other sounds in the world.

In one international conference after another, the have-not nations --- referred to as LDCs or Less Developed Countries in diplomatic circles --- have zeroed in on the U.S. with demands for a fair share of our wealth and resources.

It didn't matter what subject each conference addressed. The nations met in Stockholm to talk about the environment, in Bucharest to talk about over-population, in Rome to talk about food and starvation, in Paris to talk about energy, in Caracas to talk about the law of the sea....

Wherever they met, the LDCs began singing their new theme song --- "We Want Our Share" --- and drowned out all attempts to resolve the conference issues. Now they say they have a moral and legal right to a portion of all our natural wealth.

What kind of a monster have we created? The nations we have been helping --- and draining ourselves to do it --- are turning on us, the hand that fed them. No other nation in world's history has provided as much food, monetary, and health aid to other nations, big and small. We have worked ourselves into a crisis of inflation, food and energy shortages, and a lopsided economy through sending our produce and materials, as well as our science, technology, and cash, to underdeveloped and developed nations alike.

Perhaps some of the programs we initiated have not been successful. Maybe some of them were self-serving or poorly managed. But who can say what the condition of the world might be today if we had not poured out the billions of dollars annually in our resources and cash to needy nations since the Second World War?

Little wonder that many responsible Americans are turning a deaf ear to the Roar of the Mouse and taking stock of our remaining resources and production abilities and our future role in the world. We must hope that the pendulum won't swing too far in the direction of isolation, but it is clear a "reappraisal" is in order.

The U.S. must begin asking questions of its own. How many people in the world are there to be fed? Can we go on trying to do it all without risking exhaustion of our own resources --- and a national calamity? Does the Earth have enough arable land to raise food for the booming populations?

Then we have a truly big one: Can we, with a declining birth rate, go on sustaining countries that will do nothing about their booming birth rate --- but which keep insisting we have a duty to feed and clothe them?

Despite the fact that the U.S. has finally arrived at the zero birth-rate level, we have to look at these future statistics: In another decade or so, the U.S. will experience a 25 percent increase in its work force, a 34 percent increase in households and a 61 percent (!) jump in persons between the ages of 25 and 35.

Obviously, we will have a growing economy. We must

have. How will those needs affect our ability to play the benevolent uncle to the rest of the world?

In the meantime, the birth rates continue skyrocketing in all but a few nations. Anyone can see that some hard, even cruel decisions lie ahead. Science and technology can help find new ways to increase the supplies of food and materials, but the Earth's supply is limited. And so should be our generosity.

Science is discovering ingenious ways to extract foodstuffs from the land, from the sea, and through imaginative preservative methods. And some day, the world's political leaders will recognize the potential of the tropics --- those vast, untapped, lush lands --- for producing food.

Despite all that, the critical questions of food supply and overpopulation can never be answered by science and technology alone. Nature has had a way of resolving such problems cruelly with plagues and floods and other catastrophes, but man is gradually conquering them, too.

Only calm, orderly, determined decisions by nations meeting in earnest cooperation will solve the dilemma through positive political action. It's time for the U.S. to inform the world we will dance no longer to the Roar of the Mouse.

CHAPTER 11
A PERMANENT END TO ENERGY CRISES

*I*t saddens me to recall that the greatest contribution Dr. Ray tried to make to the nation she loved so much was shelved in the nation's capital --- and still resides there. It was a well researched and organized proposal she offered President Nixon to end energy crises for all time and render the U.S. free of any reliance on foreign nations for fuel to power the economy.

***

To paraphrase the philosophers, it is wise to study the past in order to make the important decisions of the future. I can think of no better example of that wisdom than to recall a crucial event --- or perhaps I should say non-event --- in American history.

In the last quarter of the 20th Century, the nation came upon the most serious energy crisis it has known in three centuries. In fact, that crisis is still with us, even though few will acknowledge it. The U.S. and Western European nations found themselves in the grip of Middle Eastern oil barons, who dictated the amount of oil that could be purchased, as well as the purchase price. We could only blame ourselves for not drilling for more oil within our own lands and, even more important, for not researching and developing other energy resources.

Political events both at home and abroad played a significant role. For example, it could be said that the severe energy crisis was a belated casualty of the Watergate Scandal --- and perhaps its worst casualty. I witnessed that tragedy firsthand.

On June 29, 1973, President Nixon sent a directive to me as chairman of the U.S. Atomic Energy Commission, asking me "to undertake an immediate review of federal and private energy research and development activities." He wanted me and the Energy Policy Office to come up with a program that would ensure "energy self-sufficiency" for America for centuries ahead.

Americans who were driving automobiles in 1973 will remember the gasoline shortage and the long lines at the pumps that year. Motorists across the country were angry over the cutbacks imposed by foreign oil-producing nations, and the President was convinced that "self-sufficiency" in all forms of energy was the proper goal.

Nixon told me he wanted my "recommendations for energy research and development programs" on his desk by December 1, 1973. His goal was to "include the proposals in his fiscal year 1975 budget."

Just 12 days earlier --- June 17, 1973 --- five burglars from Nixon's Committee to Re-elect the President were seized by police as they attempted to bug the Democratic National Committee's offices at the Watergate complex in the national capital. Nixon brushed off reports of the incident and insisted he and the White House had nothing to do with the burglary. In fact, the voting public must have believed him, because he was re-elected to a second term in November of that year.

However, that attitude changed abruptly when the public learned the truth about Watergate. Nixon and his administrative cohorts did, indeed, know about the break-in and had a hand in planning it.

In the meantime, I assembled an impressive group of public and private scientists, engineers, chemists, and others from several governmental agencies and scores of private industries and university faculties. The voluminous, well-researched report I took to the President in the Oval Office on December 3, 1973, was titled "The Nation's Energy Future."

When I approached the President, who sat slumped at his desk, I was alarmed by how much he had aged since I had seen him at cabinet meetings "before the Watergate reports hit the fan." He seemed "like a Zombie, trying hard to seem interested but already a defeated man."

Nevertheless, I proceeded to hand him the report and to explain its contents in short, simple language. Although he was not the Nixon of old, he managed to indicate fleeting interest in what I was saying. After all, the report had been his idea.

I was immensely proud of the report, which I told him was undoubtedly one of the most scholarly and extraordinarily well researched reports ever produced by government. It proposed a five-year program, costing $10 billion, based on these five main proposals:
1. Conserve energy by reducing consumption and conserving energy resources by increasing the technical efficiency of conversion processes.
2. Increase domestic production of oil and natural gas as rapidly as possible.
3. Increase the use of coal, first to supplement and later to replace oil and natural gas.
4. Expand the production of nuclear energy as rapidly as possible, first to supplement and later to replace fossil energy.
5. Promote, to the maximum extent feasible, the use of renewable energy sources (hydro, geothermal, solar) and pursue the promise of fusion and central station solar power.

The report went into detail on how each task was to be approached. It also

Included a timetable for the accomplishment of each task within the five-year program proposed. At the same time, it offered a step-by-step blueprint of programs to come in the years after the implementation of the initial $10 billion national program.

Throughout the report, the importance of conservation and preservation of the environment was spelled out.

As careful as I could, I cautioned the President to avoid insisting on "self-sufficiency" as an energy policy. I told him that goal was not attainable realistically and that, in fact, it might not be advisable in view of America's need to pursue a global strategy in politics and economics, as well as in the pursuit of enough energy to satisfy the nation's needs.

The primary goal, I emphasized, was to end America's dependency upon oil from foreign nations. That, I said with reference to statements made by the scientists who had helped write the report, should be the initial target.

Through it all, I had the distinct impression that the President was listening only sporadically and that nothing I was saying was registering on his mind. His expressionless face created a shudder in my spine. Was the monumental research undertaken in the previous six months wasted?

Nixon mumbled a thank-you, and I left the Oval Office, now convinced that his haggard look indicated his mind was on Watergate and not the energy crisis of 1973. My fears were substantiated a short time later, when it was disclosed that Nixon had not only known about the break-in but had authorized his former attorney general, John Mitchell, to proceed with it.

My report was consigned to the shelf as Nixon's demeanor and his presidency collapsed. The report he had demanded was never presented to the cabinet, the administration, nor Congress. As far as I know, it still sits on a shelf in the Energy Department office. In the meantime, anti-nuclear forces wore down many key members of Congress, and my exceptional research agency, the U.S. Atomic Energy Commission, was abolished in favor of a politically harmless Energy Department.

A couple years later, another "energy report" was produced for congressional viewing, but it was so limited in scope that it, too, was consigned to the shelf.

If my report, "The Nation's Energy Future," had been presented to Congress by the President --- any President --- and made the law of the land, California, Oregon, Washington, and, soon, all other states of the Union would not now be considering blackouts, more fuel imports, energy rations, higher taxes, and horrendous increases in all types of fuel and energy.

Is there a lesson to be learned in all this? Yes, but not until the American public has paid enormously in the wallet!

A final question: Is "The Nation's Energy Future" still valid and worth reviving and pursuing? The answer: Most assuredly! It is far more detailed and scientifically valid than other energy proposals now being considered by Congress and the White House! The President and congressional leaders would do themselves and the nation a gigantic favor if they would simply dust off the shelved report and adopt its major provisions.

One more monumental advantage would be ours if the report were adopted: Energy independence would permit us to end a reliance on oil from those nations that harbor and protect terrorists whose stated aim is to "kill Americans and reduce the U.S. to ashes." In other words, it would be a strategic defense measure for all time.

CHAPTER 12
NEWS MEDIA SHAKEUP OVERDUE

*I**n her days as a marine biologist, teacher, and director of the Pacific Science Center in Seattle, Dr. Ray was immensely popular, particularly with members of the news media. But when she went into public service and the media discovered she was a staunch Conservative, most of the print and broadcast reporters became disenchanted and extremely critical of her. What had happened was obvious, as she explained.*

***

It is now widely accepted by the press and consequently by much of the general public that man's industrial activities are "fouling our nest" and pose a threat to the total life of Planet Earth, a threat that grows more ominous year by year. Is this "conventional wisdom" correct? And what role have the news media played in perpetuating the "fouling" theme?

The risk one runs in challenging this widely held belief is the risk of being judged an apologist for industry, or, worse, to be accused of favoring pollution. Now, my disclaimer: I am not in the pay of nor employed by any industry, and I am as much opposed to pollution as anyone.

But I do part company with alarmists who misuse science to foment fear and who clamor with increasing stridency that industrial progress must stop or be re-directed into uneconomic alternatives because the world is going to pot. Is it?

In my home state of Washington, tucked into the far Northwest of the U.S., we enjoy the greatest geographical diversity of any of the 50 states, even though we are, geographically, the smallest state west of the Mississippi River. And we grow and market as many apples as all the other states combined. Apple-growing is a multimillion-dollar business.

Came the day not too long ago that the apple business collapsed. The losses in one year alone exceeded $100 million. What happened?

It was a market collapse. Orders were cancelled and people stopped buying apples because of a report issued to the press in New York City by the organization known as the Natural Resources Defense Council (NRDC).

The press release coincided with the CBS program, "60 Minutes." American apples are contaminated with a "chemical" called alar, the report claimed, and so did CBS and "60 Minutes" to their eternal shame. The report went on to warn that small children eating applesauce and drinking apple juice were being exposed to an intolerable risk of contracting cancer!

The evidence was sketchy. The NRDC declared that residues in fractions of a part per billion were found and that alar, or its breakdown product, might cause cancer in mice. The NRDC is not a scientific organization. It is a "watchdog society" of lawyers, whose main purpose is to litigate charges against high-technology industries. As an "expert" on alar in apples and on pesticides in general, the NRDC produced a Hollywood actress named Meryl Streep, who was also head of a new NRDC sub-organization called Mothers and Others Against Pesticides.

Responsible nutrition scientists with the Food and Drug Administration and the EPA all countered the NRDC claims and pointed out that:

- Alar is not a pesticide; it is a growth regulator.
- Only a fraction of the U.S. crop was sprayed.

- The NRDC tested only a few apples.
- The mouse experiments were flawed and inconclusive; mice are not "little men and women."
- To consume enough alar in residue on sprayed apples to risk cancer, one would have to eat at least 28,000 pounds of apples. And that would likely have other more immediate consequences!

Even the prestigious National Academy of Science (NAS) refuted the NRDC claim. But the damage had been done. Moreover, neither the news media nor the general public was able to judge the difference in competence and credibility between the respected scientists of NAS and the lawyers with a cause of NRDC.

For the growers of apples, this episode, which created unnecessary fear over a truly minute risk, was a severe economic setback. But for agriculture as a whole the result may be more serious. Many apple farmers in Washington switched to "organic" growing methods, with the result that their apples would be more expensive and of a lower quality.

The alar case is just one more case of a victory of hysteria over reason. Should this condition spread to other foods and other pesticides and herbicides under the slogan of banning chemicals in our food, the results could be serious indeed.

Perhaps it's time for chemists to turn their attention to detailed analysis of the things used in growing "natural" or "organic" food. It would be interesting to see what could be found, in parts per million, billion, or trillion in mulch, horse manure, and other "natural" fertilizers used in organic farming.

It is an uncontested fact that in highly technical, industrialized societies, people are healthier and live longer. The NRDC is trying to change that with simplistic, unscrupulous scare tactics. Who speaks for science?

Now, let me get to another major point in all this. The news media, print and broadcast, could prevent these false alarms and irresponsible reports from gaining the public's eyes and ears if they would quit accepting as gospel every charge they receive from the extremist environmental organizations.

It should have been the duty of the news media, for example, to dig into the alar news and discover that reputable scientists in and out of the government dismissed the NRDC charge before the damage was done to the farmers and the public.

I think the publishers, station owners, and executives of all print and broadcast media should examine the reliability of their reporters to write and broadcast the truth. At the same time, they should take a close look at reliable research that has indicated that at least 80 percent of reporters in the American news media acknowledge they are liberals or ultraliberals and are inclined to let their ideological prejudices influence their reports --- and to side with the loud and irresponsible extremist environmental organizations.

Let me go further. University and college presidents with jurisdiction over journalism or communications colleges should examine the curricula and the faculty members to make certain that only *objective reporting* is being taught. I've been told by reliable sources that many college journalism and broadcast teachers preach and teach "activist reporting" and that reporters have the right and responsibility to insert their own prejudices in their articles. To me that is inexcusable and a despicable abuse of the role of the teacher and the school. Yet, the newspapers and TV and radio stations that hire these graduates do nothing about the built-in ideologies and prejudices.

Little wonder that the public has been increasingly attracted to Conservative columnists and TV/Radio broadcasters.

I think it's time for the public to inform publishers and owners of TV and radio stations that they want balanced news and an end to liberal slants disguised as news reporting.

Perhaps in addition to the Supreme Court of Science I proposed in an earlier chapter we should consider the creation of a Supreme Court of News Reporting!

CHAPTER 13
THE GREATEST THREAT TO AMERICA

*I*f America is in jeopardy from an enemy, whether unseen or clearly visible, Dr. Ray believed strongly that we need not look abroad for the greatest danger to our future. She and I agreed to the letter with the opinion she expressed in this message, and we talked about it again and again because of its great importance. Will the nation wake up to the danger before it is too late?

***

Yes, America is in serious and increasing danger. But the projected mortal enemy won't be found in any foreign land. The enemy is among us every day of the year --- and is lodged within our borders. It is so close that many of our naïve and unsuspecting citizens cannot recognize it or they refuse to do so because they may be one of them.

That enemy goes by several names, and I must spell a few of them in capital letters to make my point: BIG GOVERNMENT, WELFARE STATE, SOCIALISM, and others.

Our Founding Fathers created history's greatest document with the U.S. Constitution, which they intended to be the eternal guardian of our liberty and our freedom. They very carefully spelled out guarantees of individual rights, as well as the rights of each state, cautioning against usurpation of individual and states' rights by the federal government.

For about a century and a half, those rights remained unsullied, and the federal government observed the delicate balance with the states and with private citizens. But the worm turned with the advent of the Great Depression in the 1930s and a serpent by the name of the New Deal upset the delicate balance, insisting that the economic crisis demanded action by the national government.

Because he was viewed as the savior of the nation with his Socialist-oriented welfare and labor programs, President Roosevelt, the father of the New Deal, was hailed as a hero by many workers, newly empowered labor-union leaders, and most of the news media. At one point, he hinted that all New Deal measures were of a temporary nature and would or should be repealed when the crisis had passed.

Eventually, the crisis ended, but the Socialist measures remained and, in fact, were strengthened and extended with the advent of President Johnson and his Great Society. One by one, the federal government gradually took over programs that should have been operated or created by the states or the private sector. The federal government bureaucracy has since grown to gigantic proportions and the national debt has grown to monstrous proportions accordingly. Contributing to a threatening economic disaster in the 21st Century is the specter of national bankruptcy, leading to a dictatorship and eventually to a Socialist state.

Hanging in the balance is the nation's historic reliance on a vigorous capitalist system and free enterprise.

Some unthinking persons have complained that capitalism is heartless and conducive to widening the gap between the haves and the have-nots. Do they believe that Socialism, the antithesis to the capitalist system, is based on human kindness?

They should compare the lot of the everyday citizen in any Socialist country with that of the average American, then decide on their relative worth and, yes, the moral superiority of the economic systems --- Capitalism versus Socialism.

If that comparison doesn't prove convincing, consider the overwhelming number of migrations to the U.S. every year with the numbers of persons --- if any --- trying to get into Socialist or Communist countries.

Capitalism is a system for creating wealth. It isn't perfect, but it has served a free America well and is becoming more and more attractive to nations of the Pacific, Southeast Asia, and the Far East.

More than two centuries ago, America embarked on a unique experiment in self-government that led to the development of the greatest and finest system the world has ever known. This did *not* come about through government benefits or entitlements and the plunder of natural resources, although the land has been used. Our nation grew and prospered because our government once was based on the fundamental belief in three ideas: Individual liberty, personal responsibility, and private ownership of wealth, including property, all resting on an economic system of capitalism.

What happened, then, with the imposition of the New Deal and the Great Society? Self-serving interests from corporations, foundations, trade associations, unions, citizens for this or that, and even welfare-rights organizations soon found it easy to play off different congressmen and even state legislators against each other as the distinctiveness in their recently expanded responsibilities became blurred.

The judiciary also stepped in, with even the federal courts taking over supervision of operations in areas as diverse as prisons, bussing of school children, extending the benefits of free education and welfare to non-citizens, and fishing for salmon in the Western states.

In the meantime, ask yourself: How many personal liberties have I lost in the process?

Even more critically, the federal government has gradually, over the course of the past five or six decades, taken over the role and responsibilities of the states, thus reversing the intent of the Constitution and our Founding Fathers. And so the federal government has grown from a small beginning to a point at which estimates now place the number of people on the federal payroll directly and indirectly at close to 20 million! And it is tremendously costly. It has grown beyond manageable size and now has a momentum of its own.

What is the awesome result today? We are run, in effect, by a gigantic conglomeration of federal bureaucracies, which regulate everything we do. They go beyond legal boundaries as they write regulations that go beyond and even distort the intent of laws written by the Congress. Call it what you will; I call it what it has actually become: Socialism. We are already in a welfare state and don't realize it!

What must we do to turn the tide and rescue the free-enterprise, capitalist system that made America great? There is only one answer and it is this:

America must undertake a massive system of privatization to ward off advancing Socialism and return the nation to its free-enterprise, capitalistic beginnings. We must regain power from the bureaucrats and Socialists and return that power to the people and to local government, where the people can watchdog its every action. In other words, we must regain our freedom from the governmental monster and restore the rights mandated in our federal Constitution.

I know from bitter experience that the Socialist bug has also bitten most of the states, and they, too, have fallen victim to the creation of large, unwieldy, inefficient, and terribly costly bureaucracies that take their cues from their federal cousins.

Now, it stands to reason that our economic system, like any other, must operate within a framework of government. Therein lies the problem. While preserving the semblance and form of our Constitution, we have moved a long way toward changing the structure of our government.

Although we make much of the separation of powers among the three branches of government, we now have a legislative branch (Congress) that is a full-time body, extending its activities far beyond the lawmaking and taxing functions originally allocated to it. And the excesses continue to grow. Will we have the courage and ability to effect total privatization before it is too late?

We are not a democracy, although too many of our citizens insist on calling us that. We are a _Republic!_ Our government should act _for_ us through our duly elected representatives. Does it?

Who governs for you? How well do you know who represents you and votes on important issues that affect your life, your livelihood, and your future? Would you willingly have your senator or representative handle your business affairs or trust him or her with your family finances? If your answer is "No," then you've elected the wrong person!

On the other hand, is it your elected senator or representative making the rules you eventually have to live by, or is it some unidentified bureaucrat who is stretching the law to his own advantage?

I have already strongly advocated a program of total privatization. Now, let me propose another blockbuster that is bound to upset virtually every politician in America:

I believe every elective office in America --- whether federal, state, or local --- should be limited to a six-year term and that no officeholder should be permitted to run for re-election. Furthermore, I believe the voters who put the official in office should have the authority to recall him at any time --- without cause! We have no shortage of potential candidates for every office, so that should not produce a hardship. It has been my experience that most shenanigans, self-serving actions, or even dishonest acts are committed by officials who have been in office a long time --- too long a time.

Finally, I would like to see a real revolution in political campaigning in America. First, I believe our laws should be amended to permit the filing of a suit against any candidate who commits libel or slander against another candidate or anyone else during a campaign. If he or she loses the lawsuit, the offending candidate would be disqualified as a candidate or, if already in office, removed from that office!

Second, I hope the day will come when we ban campaign

funds from any source and require all the news media to permit equal time and space to candidates for office. I can already hear the howls of anguish from the media executives!

And, finally, third, I would try to limit all campaigns to just a few weeks --- and no more. What a relief that would be for the besieged public!

Have I asked for too much? Hardly. The stakes are sky high. If we don't take action to right the ship of state and return power and authority to the people --- as originally ordered by Our Founding Fathers --- we may soon see the demise of the American Republic, and with it the end of freedom and liberty worldwide.

CHAPTER 14
TWO-PARTY SYSTEM FALLING APART

*C*ontributing to the danger of advancing Socialism in the U.S., in Dr. Ray's opinion, was a severe structural and ideological change in the traditional and historic two-party system. We both believed it to be a major cause of the political events that brought on the menacing welfare state and advancing Socialism.

***

Perhaps the most important element in the early development of the U.S. as history's finest Republic was the shaping of the two-party system, which was a natural outgrowth of the Constitution and its creation of a representative government answering to the people.

Although party names changed now and then in early American history and third parties rose and disappeared in short order, the nation soon settled down into the two-party system that served us well --- until the middle of the 20th Century. An examination of party history indicates clearly that the two major political parties, Democratic and Republican, may have disagreed on some issues over the years. But they maintained similar ideologies and obeyed the tenets of the Constitution.

They may have disagreed vehemently with each other

during campaigns and in congressional and legislative sessions, but their ideologies --- and their platforms --- were similar and consistent with the free-enterprise, capitalist system that made America great.

With the advent of the Great Depression in the 1930s, a serious division *split* the two major parties, fed by the Socialist-tainted legislation fostered by the New Deal. The primary rupture came in the clash between increasingly powerful labor unions and management. At the same time, the social legislation sponsored by the New Deal and the Democratic Party enveloped every other phase of American life --- from agriculture and industry to the professions.

Government began its takeover of control of many facets of private business and industry, as well as the rights the Constitution had awarded the states, including education, the professions, health, and virtually every other activity of daily life.

As the division took hold, Democrats aligned themselves with labor and the Republicans with management, although both argued they were partial to both sides. Soon the division came to have new designations. The Democrats identified themselves with Liberalism and the Republicans with Conservatism.

I am inclined to call up an old exclamation and shout, loudly and clearly, *"A pox on both their houses!"*

Both political parties have tarnished the designations, Liberal and Conservatism. The Liberalism --- or Ultra-liberalism --- the Democrats have espoused in the past half century is not the Liberalism I understood and respected in the years before the Great Depression. The new "Liberalism" preaches growth of the welfare state and control of virtually every phase of our existence by the federal government; it goes by another despicable name, no matter how much they may protest. And that name is Socialism!

The Republicans, on the other hand, have done similar damage to the once worthy cause of Conservatism. While the Democrats have moved far to the Left politically, the

Republicans have sullied the meaning of Conservatism by sliding far to the Right. I won't call it Fascism, but it may be just as dangerous in the long run.

As a result of the growing division, the two major parties have paved the way for the emergence of one or more Third Parties. That could be disastrous to the political future of America. The histories of the world's dictatorships or Socialist nations demonstrate that the breakdown of those societies came with the birth of numerous competing political parties and the resulting chaos.

How do we get back on track in the U.S. and derail the dash toward Socialism? The people should insist on a restructuring of both major parties. Democratic leaders should examine their party's platforms and principles and seriously consider the move toward privatization. Only the Democrats themselves can effect that important change in policy. The Republicans can't and wouldn't do it for them. The Democrats must roll back the governmental process and return control of the economy and everything else to the states and to the private sector.

I cannot emphasize this principle enough: Government's role is _not_ to run every phase of the economy; its role should be reserved to acting as a referee and watchdog to see to it that laws and regulations are obeyed. In addition, the federal government's role is to guarantee the nation's defense and security.

On the other hand, I hope the Republicans will examine their platforms and principles, too, and stop the drift to the Far Right. The First Amendment protects the right of all Americans to practice whatever religion they choose; it does not give religious groups the right to dictate the behavior and actions of those who may not be religious or who practice a different faith.

I suppose what I'm really saying is that I dream of a meeting of minds by the leaders of both political parties and a move toward obeying the philosophies implicit in the Constitution. They need to study American history and erect safeguards against drifts to the Far Left and the Far Right.

CHAPTER 15
THE TEACHER SPEAKS HER MIND

Dr. Ray loved her role as a scientist and cherished it, but I believe she was even more at home as the superb teacher she was most of her life. I think she was fondest of her frequent appearances as a lecturer to large national groups of college administrators and teachers. This is an example of her challenge to them --- made often the last 35 years of her life. It was first issued in the late 1970s; it should be noted that the tuition figures represented date back to that period and have since escalated markedly.

***

    I doubt that this nation has ever experienced a time in which more sensitive and critical decisions need to be made to strengthen our public and private colleges and universities --- and, in many instances, to save them from deterioration or extinction.

    Because we are in a period of great tension in all phases of education, the roles of administrators and teachers have become crucial. The decisions they make will not only affect their institutions but the entire fabric of American education and, consequently, every facet of our society. I hope this realization causes them to be firmer and bolder and more determined in decision-making.

If I can persuade them in any direction, let it be this: Whether they make the right or wrong decision is almost inconsequential alongside the worst choice: No decision at all. We are at that point in time in which the public will absolutely not accept what a Hollywood wag once described as a "definite maybe." If the people cannot expect leadership and a clear course from college administrators and faculty, from whom will they get it?

Speaking of a "definite maybe," I am convinced this is not the time for the Hamlets among us to be given the ball in higher education. Having been through the political house of mirrors and obstacle course in recent years (as Governor of Washington), I now recognize the perils of hesitation and recommend you to Polonius, rather than Hamlet, and "to thine own self be true."

Of course, I would have you listen to Polonius' advice, not to follow his course. But, then, that's what often happens to those who try to hide. A moment ago, I almost referred to the political arena as a "No Man's Land," but thought better of it upon reflection. Believe me, in politics, you can't hide behind "gender," either, as I have discovered lately.

This is a time for courage, then. It is a time for all of us --- the educators, governors, and lawmakers of this land --- to become more inquisitive and more alert to what the schools are teaching and what they are not teaching. It is a time for you to put your foot down, if you must, and make some sensible determinations about what belongs in the curriculum and what does not.

Are we afraid to make these choices? And, if we are afraid, why are we? Have we weighed the damage of risking some positive decisions and a bold course?

I must make myself clearly understood. I am most definitely _not_ advocating that educators begin meddling in the curricula for the sake of meddling. None of us is interested in chasing phantoms or apparitions --- as Hamlet did --- for the sake of controversy or political whim.

In no way am I suggesting that educators insert themselves

into a debate over the quality or quantity of courses in the physical and natural sciences, literature, the humanities, the arts, and other basic disciplines. I *am suggesting* that educators become aware of what their institutions are teaching and what they *may not realize* they are teaching. May I offer a pithy example, one of many?

I have here an advertisement from one of the newspapers in my state, and I know most educators have seen similar, or worse, examples in their own areas. The ad is about two and a half inches deep and three columns wide, easily found and read by anyone who is capable of finding and reading. In rather large type at the top of the ad we read:

"NEED A WEEKEND AWAY WITH YOUR CONVIVANT, MARRIED OR NOT?"

By the way, convivant, a rather intriguing word unto itself, is misspelled, which should tell us something about those who placed this ad for one of our large universities.

The ad goes on: "Spend prime time and energy with your partner in a secluded setting revitalizing your relationship. Life planning for couples is an opportunity to mutually examine (note the split infinitive) values and goals as separate persons and as part of a pair. Explore expectations for each other as men and women plan ways to achieve personal and mutual goals and deepen communications for intimate relationships."

Then the date and hours of "the course" are given, along with the telephone number at the university. Finally comes the irony of ironies: The price of "the course" is $101 for "double occupance," to use the gentlest euphemisms. That's $1 more than is being charged by private entrepreneurs in the city who provide similar "instruction." Is this what universities are for?

The possible benefits, social overtones, or propriety of such a course are not the issue. What you have to ask yourself, as I have, is this: Is this the kind of course I can defend as a legitimate addition to the curriculum of my college or university, for whose integrity and educational effectiveness I am responsible? Can anyone defend such a course before any individual or group, most notably those who support education through taxation or contributions?

Must colleges and universities provide all things to all men and women? Where do we draw the line? What I am saying is that no one seems to be willing to risk drawing the line anywhere in academia, despite the fact that the American public is very definitely informing us in many ways that it must be done. Our educators alone have the authority and the opportunity to do it, and they must do it.

It is an awesome responsibility, but I must add this caution: Failure to do it will invite a far greater menace to higher education. As I once advised some political opponents who shed large tears over an unusual action I had taken: "Have a Kleenex. Then take two aspirin and go to bed. You'll feel better in the morning."

It is also time that we all take a deep breath, steel ourselves, and say to the nation: "Higher education is a privilege, not a right." We should say it again and again, despite the thousands of words, placards, protesting picket lines, or what-have-you to the contrary.

I would like dearly to know who it was that invented the notion that higher education is a service or commodity the American citizen must support endlessly without a whimper of protest or a single suggestion for improvement, pruning, or greater responsiveness to the basic needs of our people.

Perhaps even more importantly, I would like to know how we got to the present-day condition, in which the legislatures of our 50 states are so thoroughly intimidated that they don't dare raise tuition or fees or put some desperately needed restraints on spending and curriculum --- and eliminate courses that seek to improve your weekends with your "convivant, married or not."

Those who represent public institutions have more soul-searching to do than their colleagues in the private field. I note with the greatest concern that many of our public institutions of higher learning are foraging increasingly in those fiscal fields, wherein the money trees grow and which once nurtured the healthiest private educational system in the world.

I am not suggesting that educators at public institutions withdraw immediately and slash their wrists, but I am asking that they consider the probable effects of proliferating direct competition with private institutions and private enterprise. Obviously, I don't have to remind them of the profound value to this nation of our privately operated and financed institutions of higher education.

What will happen to these private colleges and universities if we don't reduce and restrain the efforts that are depriving them of seed and sunlight? I needn't draw anyone pictures showing what will happen to public higher education if private higher education should vanish.

I suppose it must be clear to anyone that I don't hold a sentimental or romantic view of higher education. Frankly, I hope the word, "sensible," better describes my outlook. Like so many others in education, I had to work my way through school --- all the way through to the day the doctorate was finally in hand. I don't think much of those old-timers or new-timers, for that matter, who had only to write home for more dough so they could complete their four-year loaf.

All of which brings me to that fearsome word, "tenure." Webster defines it as "the act, right, manner, or term of holding something (as a landed property, a position, or an office). Grasp and hold."

I submit that the word "tenure" has outlived its usefulness in the lexicon of higher education. What other profession or industry guarantees lifetime employment and security, no matter how the person involved behaves, teachers, or preaches, and what he or she advocates? We have to go to nations embracing the caste system or early primitive societies to find a parallel --- or to our hallowed halls of higher education.

It is the responsible administrators and educators who feel most keenly and sensitively the pains of tenure. The system deprives them of one of the most important management tools they need to operate wisely and fairly for the entire college and university community they serve. In order to maintain sensible and efficient standards of governance, they must have the management tool of "flexibility" ---flexibility in decision-making, flexibility in administrative practices, and the most important flexibility of all: The right to change one's mind and keep pace with the essential needs of a thriving, volatile society.

In more than three decades as a teacher and some six years as a state and federal government executive, I've been asked this question again and again:

"If you are opposed to tenure as presently practiced, what do you offer as an alternative?"

My answer has always been the same: What's wrong with the historic American system of contracts and our tradition of insuring that they are fair, valid, and binding on the signatories? The validity of contracts is at the base of our free republic. If it has been good enough for the most remarkable democratic republic the world has known, is it not also good enough for our colleges and universities?

What's wrong with writing contracts that specify basics, time, substance, and other requirements? What is so sacrosanct about any teacher in higher education that he or she need not answer to the society that needs his or her teaching talent and pays the bills to utilize it? Why is the tenured faculty member in higher education privileged to live beyond the rules of responsibility all the rest of our citizens must observe? Is tenure any less offensive than the old monarch's "droit de roi" --- or "right of kings"?

More important things should be engaging our attention. For example, no one needs a computer or a swami to learn that tenure, coupled with the shrinking enrollment figures in higher education, is closing out the new, young blood our institutions must have to thrive and survive. I'm talking about those young teachers who are not only exceptionally well qualified but anxious to teach.

The other day I learned in a report in the <u>Wall Street Journal</u> that we have a growing population of what the researcher called "Gypsy scholars" --- highly qualified and briefly experienced young persons with doctorates, most of them, and with no place to go because of the impenetrable land of "Tenurism." Now, I suggest that this is a bonafide horror story. All of us should fix our gaze on the evils of the tenure system and what it is doing to our colleges and universities.

Unqualified, insubordinate, or incompetent teachers have no right to immunity from scrutiny by colleges and universities or by the citizens of each state. Nobody has that right in any profession or industry in a free society governed by laws and with a tradition for the sanctity of the individual and the validity of contractual agreements. I appeal to everyone in the field of education to exercise his or her responsibility and fulfill his or her trust by phasing out the tenure system.

A second question follows inevitably: Let us suppose the time arrives in which tenure is outlawed and that we have replaced it with a system of contracts openly arrived at. Who then will judge the validity of the contracts and see to it that their terms are fulfilled by both parties? That's the easiest question of all to answer: Educators do, of course --- the persons selected to watchdog and make policy for our colleges and universities. And, as in all other instances in our nation of laws, anyone involved in a contract has recourse to the courts.

I repeat: Educators should make such decisions. In our free society we must rely upon the wisdom and courage of those we choose as leaders to make decisions for all of us. And if those who lead should fail us, we simply replace them with others, as we see fit. If we cannot rely upon the wisdom and integrity of the men and women selected to govern through our college and university boards, then we should be honest enough to recognize it, junk the system and create another. In our ever more complicated society, we cannot afford to indulge in pretense and hypocrisy.

Members of college and university governing boards have the necessary credentials or they would not have been chosen. They have the authority and the responsibility, and everything they do is watched closely and scrutinized. Now all that remains is for them to follow their conscience and consummate their responsibility --- and they can do it without benefit of that weekend course with a convivant.

The fate of the great American system of public and private higher education rests upon their ability to do the job. No one else will do it for them, although I know a few legislators who might jump at the chance --- to say nothing of a few federal bureaucrats here and there who would dearly love to give the educators a hand.

A few additional problems disturb my mind. One educators must meet head-on as soon as possible, if they haven't already, is the issue of loose accreditations fostered by so-called regional councils or other organizations. As in the case of tenure, we must quit rationalizing the problem and act firmly and decisively to see to it that all education agencies or institutions attracting the public's dollar can deliver what they promise and that they meet standards the public has a right to expect.

It is degrading to the entire educational system and to the people to permit degrees or certificates or other documents to be awarded like coupons in a tabloid for inadequate or even non-existent academic work. It is the holder of the legitimate degree who is penalized, as well as the legitimate institution.

Similarly, I urge educators to look at the crazy quilt of "educational advertising," in addition to the convivial weekend come-on I have already referred to. We've all read or heard the advertisements for courses offered by colleges and universities that are many miles away when we know the very same courses are provided by schools in our own cities. And in classrooms with empty seats to boot. It doesn't make sense.

In this instance, I'm referring to the legitimate colleges and universities that are so desperate to achieve enrollment figures that they must invade the territory of other colleges and universities.

I cannot end this without a parting reference to the most disconcerting subject of all, financing our colleges and universities. In this case I will offer no philosophy or additional comment because the statistics take care of all that for me. These are figures from our own state, and I'm quite certain the story is much the same everywhere else. Perhaps it is even worse in some other states.

In Washington State a two-year community-college degree costs $3,448. The student pays only $612 of that total, while the taxpayer must provide the rest, $2,836. In the community-college area, the nonresident student pays $2,376 for that two-year degree and the taxpayer $1,072.

These figures, by the way, are all from our current biennium (in the 1970s and '80s), and they apply to our public colleges and universities. The total cost of a four-year college degree is $10,520, of which the student pays $2,400 and the taxpayer $8,120.

For a fifth year only, the student pays $675 and the taxpayer $4,125.

Let's combine the B.A. and the M.A. cost at the public college or university. The student pays $3,075 and the taxpayer $12,245.

Now, let's add to that a PhD degree. For the additional two years usually required to earn a doctorate, the student pays $1,308 and the taxpayer $12,062.

I have said nothing about the graduate programs in medicine, law, and other disciplines.

Do educators still need a cheerleader to persuade them to exercise their tremendous responsibility? They should ask themselves who is really responsible for the governance of colleges and universities. Is it the students? The faculty? The alumni? The college presidents? No. The members of the governing board are!

In order to remind ourselves once more who our bosses really are, it would be appropriate for me to conclude with a definition I once read but which is now a permanent part of the private lexicon of Dixy Lee Ray:

Taxpayers are people who don't have to take a civil-service examination to work for the government. Amen.

CHAPTER 16
ABOUT THAT DIRTY WORD: WASTE

*F*ew issues arouse as much public furore as "getting rid of waste" and "doing it through incineration." However, the issue grows more serious by the year as waste sites fill up and land for new sites vanishes, primarily through actions to protect the environment. Because nuclear waste is part of the problem, Dr. Ray became involved with the issue of solid wastes and chemical wastes early in her career.

***

There is nothing I can say or write about incineration that experts in the field do not already know. Like them, I believe that:

- The use of landfills in this country will inevitably decline and virtually disappear.
- Reduction in volume and detoxification will certainly expand.
- Interest in incineration is growing very rapidly and the technology holds great promise.
- It is even possible that waste management will become an honored and respected profession!

But with incineration, as with all other ways of handling waste, there are problems:

- A site must be found, one that will be accepted by

neighbors and agreeable to diverse groups of people, who often have conflicting interests and aims.
- An environmental-impact statement will undoubtedly have to be prepared and approved.
- Licenses and permits must be acquired.
- Transportation questions persist, involving various jurisdictions; these must be resolved.
- For incineration at sea, special loading and berthing ports and specially constructed ships are necessary; all maritime rules must be followed.

All of these necessities are confounded and delayed by inevitable public opposition. Just because a technology is good and license-able does not guarantee public approval. The answer to these vexing problems is always the same:

EDUCATE THE PUBLIC!

I have always responded with another question: HOW? Frankly, I don't believe it can be done. But I keep trying....

It seems so reasonable to conclude that once the public understands how good and safe and environmentally benign a technology is, the public will accept, if not welcome, it. It seems so reasonable to expect the public to be grateful that someone is taking responsible care of waste. Don't you believe it!

In the first place, how is the public going to know that the waste-management method --- let's say incineration --- is good and safe and environmentally benign? Secondly, will the public believe it on the sayso of experts or on mine --- assuming, of course, that we have some way to communicate directly with the public?

Third, is the waste manager a credible source of assurance to the public?

Finally, does the public think that:
- The generators of waste are credible?
- The nuclear industry is credible?
- The chemical industry is credible?
- The representatives of government agencies are credible?

- Research scientists --- or engineers --- are credible?

The course of public events, especially in nuclear science and now increasingly in the chemical industry, as well, have over the past couple decades demonstrated that none of the groups just listed are believed. The public is far more likely to believe the opponents of science and technology than to believe its supporters.

If one is reluctant to accept that proposition, consider for a moment how one would fare on "60 Minutes" or "20/20" or "Crossfire" or on any of the many TV and radio programs where controversial issues --- even highly complex technical ones --- are treated in an adversarial debate-like format, as if questions of scientific fact could be settled, not by evidence, but by argument.

I have likened this way of informing the public in scientific matters to a hypothetical situation, in which a TV broadcast program on criminal justice features a "balanced" panel made up of three judges and three criminals. That, of course, is the fairness doctrine --- presenting both sides. At least, that's the way it works in science and technology!

In such a format, the opposition always "wins," because whoever is against any technology has only to make a charge, however preposterous; he or she doesn't have to prove it. That burden falls on the supporter of science to prove that the charge is groundless. It is a difficult situation, and it is one that we handle badly.

There was a time, in the long ago of my youth, when experts were believed. It was a time when most people and most institutions were presumed to be well-meaning and honest until and unless proved to be otherwise. It was also a time of an unprecedented increase in knowledge, of belief in ourselves, and in our ability through understanding and logic to provide adequate solutions to technical problems.

It was a time of optimism and progress. It was a time of improvements in the conditions of living that made our society and our nation the envy of the world. It was a time when the use of knowledge was expected, when the myriad applications of science through technology made living on this Earth easier and better, and gave us more time to enjoy it by increasing our life span beyond three quarters of a century.

Funny thing, though. It's still that kind of time.... But it seems that hardly anyone enjoys it any more!

Too many people have exchanged confidence for despair, too many have come to fear technology and to hate and reject anything nuclear or chemical. Despite all the evidence of physical well-being beyond the dreams of all previous generations, we seem to have become a nation of easily frightened people and the healthiest hypochondriacs in the world!

What has brought this condition about? What has made us rather lament than rejoice, quick to believe the worst about ourselves and reluctant to recognize the good that exists so abundantly around us? Among other possible explanations, we've just done a rotten job of teaching science. Oh, not to those students who will become scientists ---we're quite good at that --- but at the equally important job of teaching science to all those others, the 80 percent or so of the student population who will not enter science or engineering as a profession. There we fail miserably.

And so we must ask the further question: If not from the schools and colleges, where do most people (the "public") get their information about science and about important applications of technology in modern society? The answer is easy. They get it mainly from TV and, to a lesser extent, from newspapers, radio, and news magazines. And who decides what this information is? Not scientists, but reporters, news directors, and editors.

Professor John Kemeny, chairman of the President's Inquiry into the accident at Three Mile Island, commented this way after dealing with the press about his report:

"I left Washington fully expecting to read the following story some day in one of our morning newspapers: 'Three scientists named Galileo, Newton, and Einstein have concluded that the Earth is round. However, The New York Times has learned authoritatively that Professor John Doe of Podunk has conclusive evidence that the Earth is flat.'"

If we want a public better educated in science and, therefore, more competent to make rational decisions (meaning to agree with us?!!) on technical matters that affect them, then we must understand better the different worlds in which scientists and reporters live and work.

We have to recognize that scientists (and technologists and engineers) do not and cannot inform the public directly. The media inform the public. And in doing so, the media act as an information filter. The bottom line is that science and the news media must learn to work together for a common purpose, because there is simply no other mechanism that can provide the necessary scientific information to society for social decision-making. So far, this rapport between science and the media shows no signs of developing.

Consider the differences in the way of working, the motivations, and the rewards for scientists and for reporters. First, the scientists: For them, the volume of work is far less important than its quality. Scientists work at their own pace; there is no irretractible daily or weekly deadline. Scientists work within a well recognized discipline, which is only a small part of the scientific whole. A scientist's work is judged by his peers; unless it is peer-approved, it won't be published. For a scientist, all funding and advancement is based on peer-reviewed work.

For all these reasons, scientists are very careful about making claims. Scientists who value their standing in the peer community (nothing else really matters) will be cautious not to overstate, and they will feel compelled to provide context for what they say. This is often interpreted by the non-scientific community as uncertainty, doubt, hedging, or even as evidence of disagreement among scientists.

In the news media, on the other hand, a reporter's key to advancement is the volume of his work, maximizing air-time minutes or inches of print. Competition for time and space is fierce. For the reporter, deadlines are externally imposed, are short, and must be met.

Disciplines in science are non-existent for the reporter; he must cover them all. A reporter's work is judged not by his peers, but by an editor or news director, and what attracts attention is paramount in importance. Good reporting is compact, without space for qualifications and context; on TV, 60 seconds is the usual maximum for a news report. Under such circumstances, reporters cannot read scientific papers; most of their work is done on the telephone, and they search out "experts" who will give them good one-liners.

Remember that the media are self-appointed defenders of the public faith, and most people accept them in this role. Reporters inform the public about peril, because this is what the public expects. The fastest way for a reporter to succeed and become established and recognized is to raise the specter of imminent peril and then take up the cudgels on behalf of society to deal with it.

There could hardly be two more diverse professions. Little wonder that there is both misunderstanding and misrepresentation. The good scientist strives to be precise by qualifying his statements and and staying within the context of a scientific discipline. This is usually done in a deliberate manner.

The good reporter strives for a fast response, for a compact statement that is reasonably accurate. Above all, a good reporter makes his statement in a manner designed to make the greatest impact on readers, viewers, or listeners. Therefore, information flowing from the scientific environment to the media's environment inevitably suffers alteration and filtration, and this affects public perceptions.

In another regard, there appear to be three main problems:
1. An understandable, though unfortunate, emphasis on conflict between technology and social interest makes good press, but often unnecessarily heightens anxiety. The public will accept bad news, but it has been conditioned to reject good news as whitewash.
2. The persistence of false information is made believable

by constant repetition. This leads to dissemination of what are sometimes called "Factoids," a term coined by two Canadian researchers. A factoid, they said, is a statement based on a tiny bit of evidence and a cluster of misinformation placed atop and around it. Examples of "Factoids" are:
- PCBs cause cancer.
- Any level of radiation is harmful.
- Acid rain is caused by sulfur dioxide from burning coal.

Etc., etc....There are dozens of such Factoids, beliefs that have no basis in evidence. Some come about from the mistaken belief that if two phenomena occur together or follow one another, they must represent cause and effect. Some have come from an initial distorted opinion of a scientist wanting publicity for a cause or a political position; some originate with a zealous reporter trying to get ahead in journalism.

3. Since good scientists limit their remarks within disciplinary boundaries and good reporters extrapolate into a broad or common context, the result is often *misinterpretation*. "I was misquoted," says the scientist --- and vows never to talk to a reporter again. Such a reaction is a mistake, because it leaves the field of communicating with the media open to those scientists who avoid peer review for their work, have a mission or "cause," or are charlatans or quacks. Science has its quota of the latter, just as does every profession. And it's up to good scientists to weed out these phonies. But we don't do it! Rather, by our science, we allow such renegades --- organizations like the "Union of Concerned Scientists" --- to present themselves as the "voice of the scientific community." They back up the Helen Caldicotts, Barry Commoners, Paul Ehrlichs, Amory Lovinses, and other pretenders.

While the respected scientific community judges very strictly those at the top of their profession, they simply ignore the incompetents and no-goods at the bottom. It is left to others of courage, like the Honorable Patrick F. Kelly of the

U.S. District Court in Kansas to say (November 15, 1984) what we should have been saying all along:

"This Court rejects the opinion testimony of Dr. Morgan and Dr. Gofman, because they both evidence an intellectually dishonest invention of arguments to protect their opinion.... This is not a situation where the scientific community is equally divided between two respected schools of thought. It is a case where there is a small but very vocal group of scientists, including Dr. Morgan and Dr. Gofman, that holds views not considered credible by experts in the field...."

Dr. Ernest Sternglass, much quoted by the media on radiation matters, has never published his claims about the effect of low-level radiation in a peer-reviewed journal. In an article in Esquire magazine, published in 1969, Dr. Sternglass predicted that all children in the U.S. would die as a result of fallout from nuclear tests.

Unfortunately for his credibility, but fortunately for children, he was, and is, wrong. But Dr. Sternglass' opinions, long since dismissed by knowledgeable scientists in his field, continued to be sought and quoted by the popular press.

Until respected scientists, perhaps through their professional societies or through the National Academy of Science, identify these purveyors of misrepresentation and architects of Factoids for what they are --- charlatans and quacks or incompetents --- then we have only ourselves to blame for the media quoting them in preference to those who represent the main body of science.

We should be very careful of who it is that speaks for science, because in our age of high technology, a misinformed or uninformed public can stop any project, even when it is in society's benefit.

How can the public be educated? I don't know. But of this I am certain: The public will remain uninformed and uneducated in science until news-media professionals decide otherwise.

(Note: One example among many keeps popping up in TV newscasts and in print. Reporters, anchors, and others continue to use the term, Factoids, to mean a bit of accurate news! They simply don't understand that the term originated as a description of a slim sliver of fact immersed in oodles of misinformation! Will the media ever learn? --- L.G.)

CHAPTER 17
REDISCOVERING LIVING PLANTS

One of the most ridiculous and surprising charges made against Dr. Ray by some news-media critics and extremist environmental groups was that she was anti-environment. The militants should have known better, or perhaps they didn't care that she was one of the pioneer environmentalists of the Pacific Northwest. I should know; I was her partner in the new environmental movement at the time. All doubters need to be convinced is this message delivered often by Dr. Ray.

***

Whatever happened to the Teddy Roosevelt dream of reforesting the Earth? It is more important today than ever before, and for many more reasons than Roosevelt himself imagined.

We need not only trees but plants, billions of them. And they should not be relegated to rural sites; the cities need them even more, in fact.

They aren't needed for firewood. On the contrary, Europe destroyed its great forests in earlier centuries, because it demanded and required fuel for heat. So did other continents. That day is gone, fortunately, but the need for trees and plants is greater than ever.

We must have them, not only for the wood products, paper, and other essentials they give our industries but for the life-giving values they provide. And the environmental qualities they possess in abundance, as well as the visual delights.

I do not understand why no concerted effort at reforestation has been made by the environmental forces --- nor why they haven't demanded that urban areas blanket their buildings, streets, homes, and open areas with plants and trees. Pollution, they say, is the problem. Then why not fight pollution the best way the Earth itself has shown us how to fight --- with oxygen-producing, dioxide-devouring, pollution-controlling living plants?

Plants and trees are natural air-conditioners. Yet, American cities and towns act as if they had never heard of them as pollution-fighters.

But, you say, much of the urban pollution is produced by the burning of certain types of fossil fuels that release carbon monoxide, not carbon dioxide. Nature has done it again. Some plants, like English ivy, feast on carbon monoxide, and they grow in abundance. Why not give them a chance to do the job?

Most of all, however, I am intrigued by the tremendous potential of living plants as energy producers. We tend to cultivate plants for two purposes only, food and fiber. Why not grow them on "energy farms" strictly for producing fuels?

Through bioconversion or chemical conversion, the "energy farm" plants could be turned into such fuels as methane, methanol, alcohols, and the higher synthetic fuels. This is not a pipe dream; it has already been done in the laboratory successfully and, in fact, in actual practice in a few places.

"Energy farms" were never practical when the price of petroleum was relatively low. At today's prices, however, the experimental ideas for extracting fuels from plants look good.

Maine has pioneered a program in which huge stores of pine needles, bark chips, roots, and other waste from the state's large paper industry has found good use, at last. These wastes are delivered to a new plant that turns them into methanol, which, in turn, will run the paper mills. Presto! A huge saving in fuel once purchased to operate the mills.

Every state in the nation and every country in the world has waste that could be utilized. And those that need more could plant "energy farms."

One of the experiments that has impressed me as most promising of all in this vein is a proposal by a researcher in Hawaii to use one of the most plentiful plants available --- the microscopic algae, chlorella --- to produce fuel. Chlorella grows in swimming pools, as well as standing bodies of water, and it can be grown abundantly anywhere, at any temperature.

Production estimates in this oil-short world are even more impressive. Chlorella on an "energy farm" can yield nearly 120 bushels, dry-weight, an acre, from which 86 barrels of synthetic fuels would be produced. One can see what could be done with a farm of 1,000 acres or more.

Best of all, its cost would be competitive with the price of oil at today's levels --- and tomorrow's.

A test farm and plant are needed. It's estimated the entire chlorella experiment could be consummated for $10 million. Maybe an adventurous American oil company could give it a try --- with a loan of some of that plentiful Arab money that's looking for U.S. know-how.

CHAPTER 18
ENERGY FOR THE WORLD

One of the most profound and telling addresses delivered by Dr. Ray was made to a world conference of coal producers back in the early 1980s. Understandably, her topic was the world's crucial reliance on energy, a subject that monopolized her speeches, articles, and books.

***

It is good to remind ourselves from time to time that energy and its use made industrialized society possible and is the primary ingredient to sustaining it. Energy turns the wheels of industry, as well as those of transportation. It's required for the conversion of raw materials into resources, for the production of all goods, medicines, fertilizers, for the growing of food, and for the operation of all commerce. Energy eases domestic living and powers high technology. It runs the communications systems and computers that seem increasingly to order our daily lives.

Life in industrial society is not an unmitigated good; it is just better, for more people, than any other type of society that humankind has tried. Industrialization means longer and healthier lives, means greater freedom from hard manual labor, a greater share of goods and services, and more personal freedom than any other society ever conceived.

Whether industrial society grows and prospers depends in a material sense on two things: Energy and raw materials. The availability of both raises sobering questions, which I will examine. Of course, the shape of the future depends on many other factors --- peace, freedom of speech, education, the rights of individuals and institutions, a decent standard of living, hope.... And so on.

But in a very fundamental and practical sense, *all* of these require a healthy economy or they will not long endure. And a healthy economy demands assured supplies of energy and raw materials at reasonable cost.

Since both energy and raw materials tend to be spread unequally over the world and, curiously enough, to occur in abundance mostly where people are not, this gives rise to problems that --- when they are intractable or persistent --- we call crises.

Although the history of Western civilization is replete with enough crises to keep even the most dedicated doomsayers contented, and predictions that depletion of the world's store of fossil fuels is imminent have been made repeatedly since the dawn of industrialization, we can date the current perception of a world energy crisis from 1973.

The withholding of Middle East oil from the world market and the subsequent dramatic increases in the price of petroleum were followed, in the words of Marchetti (1980) "....by an extraordinary flow of talk, papers, and adrenaline." Now, Marchetti also maintained, in the thought-provoking Bernard Gregory Lecture delivered in Geneva in November, 1980, that "....energy is not really more important than matter, and does not deserve a privileged treatment."

While I agree that energy and matter (raw materials) are equally important and interlinked and that it is not energy *per se* that has such special significance but rather what society can do with it, I also firmly believe that energy does merit "a privileged treatment," whether we think there is an energy crisis or not. Why?

Perhaps a little historical perspective will help. For 5,800 years out of the approximate 6,000 years of human civilization, most of the fossil fuels and all of the fission energy lay buried beneath the Earth's surface. Only wind, falling water, and the burning of forests augmented human and animal labor.

Eighty-some years ago --- 1900 --- in the U.S., the population numbered about 76 million persons and they used 10 quads (10/15BTU) of energy costing about $4 billion. The annual energy used per capita was 40,000 Kwh thermal, equivalent to the physical labor of 110 human slaves working eight hours a day, 365 days a year for each man, woman, and child --- and the slaves consuming no energy themselves and paid a wage of about 0.01 cents an hour! At that time 21 percent of our energy came from wood, 71 percent from coal, and about 2 percent each from oil, natural gas, and hydropower.

Now, in the 1980s, we have increased our energy use (220 million population, 80 quads energy) to the equivalent of about 300 slaves per capita, at the increased cost of about 0,1 cents per slave per hour! The energy mix has shifted so that petroleum now occupies the dominant position.

Indeed, about half the total energy used in the world today comes from oil. The price has risen from a few dollars a barrel in 1970 to $12 a barrel in 1974 and $35 a barrel by 1980. This dramatic price increase has had a significant impact in the U.S. It has reduced energy growth from 4 percent to 1.5 percent a year, increased the cost of imported supplies from $8 billion in 1973 to $100 billion today, giving us a severely negative trade balance. It has fueled inflation, reduced the Gross National Product, and resulted in serious economic recession.

Certainly there is not a one-to-one correlation between energy cost and the national economy, but there *is* a strong relationship. To sum up, energy is important and crucial to the industrialized world. The first factor in the world energy crisis is its increased cost.

Now, let's look at the importance of energy from another vantage point --- that of agriculture. Indeed, throughout much of the Third World, energy and food are synonymous. In

America, about 7 percent of the population feeds the entire nation, and one fourth of the rest of the world, as well. This situation came about through much hard work and inventiveness, making use of new technologies and machines --- all of them requiring energy.

To use just one example: In the non-industrialized world, one farmer, using only 166 mega-calories of energy, working for 1,150 hours, can produce 6,700 mega-calories of corn. By contrast, in the U.S. one farmer using 8,000 mega-calories of energy and only 17 hours of labor, can produce 18,700 mega-calories of corn --- or three times as much. Or, to look at it in a different light, one farmer in the U.S. in 1910 could feed 7.1 persons; today he feeds 59. (The world average is 5.1.)

In 1910, with a team of horses, one farmer could plow one acre a day; today, with a tractor, he plows more than 35 acres a day. In 1910, one acre of land yielded 26 bushels of corn; today the same acre yields 97. Energy makes the difference. But there are those who would have us return to pre-industrial agriculture…. What would that mean?

In the words of Eric Ruttley, secretary general of the World Energy Conference (at the Toronto meeting in 1980):

"If energy for agricultural machinery and the machinery of industry were suddenly taken away from us --- right now --- most of the world's population would have to die, not over the natural span of three-score years and 10, but quickly."

Go back to more labor-intensive farming? Nonsense. In 1910, 25 percent of the arable land had to be used to raise feed for the farm-work animals. If we were to produce _today's_ crops with pre-industrial technology, in addition to large areas set aside for animal feed, we would require in the U.S. alone more than 61 million horses and mules. Now, it would take 20 years to breed this number, since there are only 3 million alive today, and it would take an additional 27 million farm workers to take care of them!

Sensible? No. And so the second important factor in the world energy crisis is _availability_ of energy supplies --- having sufficient amounts to sustain intensive agriculture, as well as industrialization.

That brings us to the question of scarcity. Are we running out of fossil fuel? Certainly some people believe that we are entering an "Age of Scarcity."

From publications like Barbara Ward's "Spaceship Earth" to the Club of Rome's "Limits to Growth" to Amory Lovin's softheaded "soft technologies" and Paul Ehrlich's "End of Affluence," the popular press has popularized Malthusian projections of the idea of immutable limits and certain scarcity ahead.

Nor is it just the mass media wherein there is widespread belief that the future must be worse than the present; that we have reached the end of industrial progress; that we must get along with what we have, and that conservation is our only salvation. Such attitudes are also widespread among academics, especially liberal-arts faculties but including a surprising number of basic-science professors. Curious as it is, notions of inevitable decline have widespread appeal among the young, the highly educated, and the relatively well off.

Nor is this just a modern phenomenon.

In 1864, W. Stanley Jevons, one of the 19th Century's noted social scientists, wrote a carefully documented, comprehensive book predicting that England's industry would soon grind to a halt with the exhaustion of England's coal. He wrote:

"It would appear that there is no reasonable prospect of any relief from a future want of (this) main agent of industry. We cannot long continue our present rate of progress."

Jevons also believed that there was no possibility of any alternate fuel solving England's problem!

Are the modern Malthusians right? My answer is a resounding NO! I believe they take into account neither history, nor human nature, nor the stubborn diversity and sheer creativeness of the human mind. But those who preach scarcity have wide appeal, especially to the nontechnical, nonscientific public. The idea of scarce resources draws its credibility from the logic that the Earth is finite, its resources limited --- as, of course, they are!

The argument is that industrial society is using up the world's supply of stored resources at an alarming and increasing rate, and given a growing human population and continued industrialization, a point of diminishing returns has been, or soon will be, reached. What is worrisome about this thesis is the possibility that if such attitudes become widespread, the prophecy could become self-fulfilling.

Now we have the third factor in our energy crisis --- a belief that energy supplies (resources) are *scarce* and fast disappearing.

But is this belief rational? In the 1952 landmark publication, "Resources for Freedom," better known as the report of the Paley Commission, we have a good starting point for evaluating the relative scarcity or abundance of fossil fuels and other strategic materials. This remarkable government study (mercifully, it was published before the invention of bureaucratese!) projected the free world's known resources of minerals and other key commodities.

Nearly all of them have now been revised upward by amounts varying from 10 percent for tin to a whopping 43 percent for phosphates! Even oil's "known reserves" have increased 50 percent since 1952 --- not taking into account the effect of deregulation and advanced recovery techniques in the U.S. nor recent discoveries in Mexico.

Forecasting of anything is imprecise, and with the Earth's resources, the estimates will inevitably rise whenever recovery techniques improve or prices go up.

In commenting on the "Limits to Growth" in 1972, analysts from the World Bank concluded:

"We do not know the true extent of the resources that exist in, and can ultimately be recovered from, the Earth. Nor will we know in the next two years or the next ten.... We don't know, because no one has yet found it necessary to know, and therefore to make, an accurate inventory."

Today, ten years later, we can add that most of the world is *still* to be explored --- both in extension and in depth.

For purposes of demonstrating the difficulty of establishing precisely the "known reserves" of anything, let me take as an example one single metal --- copper. Expressed in terms of present "known reserves" divided by the annual rate of consumption, we get the figure of 45 years of consumption potential remaining for copper.

But if we take the U.S. Geological Survey estimate for "ultimate recoverable" copper (generally regarded as equivalent to 0.1 percent of the materials in the top kilometer of the Earth's crust), we find 340 years of consumption potential. And again --- applying the same procedure to the total amount of copper *estimated* to be *present* in the Earth's crust, the years of consumption potential rise to a staggering 242 million! How much copper is there…really? A 45-year supply? 340 years? 242 million years? That is a rather wide range! The answer depends on need, cost, and technology.

Moreover, who would have predicted a few years ago that low-grade ores could be treated, on a commercial basis, to extract metals from them? But that *is* happening, and today both copper and uranium are being recovered by leaching with bacteria, mainly of the genus Thiobacillus --- and industrial microbiology is in its infancy in this application. Who knows what process improvements may occur with genetic manipulation?

Any honest appraisal of resources, whether fuel or mineral, must conclude that they are vast, but we don't really know. Coal? Certainly there is enough for many centuries. Natural gas? The equivalent of all the oil used in Europe is flared by oil producers in the Middle East because the present cost of transportation makes marketing it unprofitable. And new theories postulate continuous formation of methane bubbling up from inside the Earth.

Oil? If heavy crudes, shale oil, and tar sands are taken into account, the reserves are enormous. What we *do* know is that the cheap, easily recoverable, rich deposits are limited and they are spotty in distribution.

Access is a more severe problem than the mere existence of the desired materials, and that is our fourth factor of world crisis in energy --- access.

Here, too, the picture is complicated by politics and governmental actions. Restrictive rules or procedures, both international and within specific countries, can render even an abundant resource essentially inaccessible. Let me use just one humble example --- drawn from an area far removed from energy --- hamburger! This ubiquitous meat in the U.S. costs 8 to 11 cents *more* per pound because it is controlled by 41,000 regulations, 200 legal statutes, and 161,000 precedent-setting court cases brought on behalf of consumers!

And, if you think hamburger is burdened with self-righteous government do-gooding, then you haven't tried to open a coal mine, built a slurry pipeline, or, heaven forbid, constructed a coal or nuclear electric power plant. Government actions, taken for political or other reasons, constitute a not inconsiderable fifth factor in the world energy crisis picture.

Finally, we come to the sixth, and I believe the last and most important factor in the world energy crisis --- public perception.

Most of the world's peoples have a standard of living that is unacceptably low and dangerously dependent upon the natural ecosystem. Improvement can come *only* with greater use of energy, coupled with a healthy, expanding economy. But here we come up against the paradox that --- at least in the industrialized countries --- those who profess to speak for the poor are almost all opponents of industrialization and against the present uses of energy. They are dedicated to stopping all growth in energy use.

Willfully ignorant of science and as distrustful of engineering as of business, these opponents view industrial society as debased by technology. Our health is being ruined, they say, by junk food, chemical preservatives, and inorganic fertilizers. Then how come people live longer and healthier in industrial societies?!

No matter. Our landscapes are despoiled and we are told that we're forced to do demeaning work and to consume unwanted products. We are being dehumanized, they say, and this is happening because a technological demon has escaped human control and because evil scientists and technocrats are leading the public astray. Nonsense!

Technology is very much under society's control. However we use technology, its course is decided by human beings. But much of the public believes otherwise. To ignore the public's perceptions and its easily aroused fears about SO2 emissions, acid rain, and CO2 accumulation in the atmosphere is to doom expanded coal use as surely as irrational fears of radiation and nuclear wastes have brought the nuclear industry to its knees.

Do not rejoice in the weakening of a competitor, because you cannot supply all of society's energy needs, and, important as it is, coal is not without its own problems of health and environmental risk.

People have come to expect that the energy companies and utilities will provide any amount of energy as a matter of right, and the more successful the energy corporations are at providing more, the less popular they get. Learn from the lesson of nuclear.

To a world that wanted electricity cheaper than it could be made from fossil fuels, nuclear supplied it. To a world that wanted electricity that did not assault the environment, nuclear supplied it. To a world troubled by occupational hazards of mining, nuclear supplied an alternative. But the public got the idea that there should be no risk.

It has become easy for people to believe, for example, that the sun is a cosmic electricity company, ready to supply us with electricity on the scale and with the efficiency of Commonwealth Edison --- and without sending us a bill, if only the energy companies weren't so greedy.

And so, to the world energy crisis factors of (1) cost, (2) availability, (3) concerns about scarcity, (4) access, and (5) governmental regulations, we have to add the final problem of public perception and the question of relative risks. To educate the public in this regard is the greatest challenge, and it constitutes the major energy crisis of our time. If you fail to educate the public --- as nuclear failed --- we are lost. If you succeed, the world is profoundly in your debt.

But do not wait for anyone to give thanks. In the real world of today, no good deed goes unpunished! The energy companies, up to now, have served society too well to escape calumny. Their work is of the utmost importance --- if we are to resolve the world's energy crisis. Good luck!

CHAPTER 19
SHORT TAKES

Dr. Ray was a woman of many interests; here is a sampling of her wisdom in a variety of fields.

***

Defense Establishment Needs Restructuring

I have always been in favor of a strong American defensive arm, but, with military technology and tactics undergoing constant change to meet future needs, I believe costs can and should be trimmed. One way would be to combine many of the units that perform similar functions in each branch --- administration and records, food supplies, uniforms and clothing, medical needs and records, basic training, and, perhaps, even ordinance and small arms. Under a single command, the military branches --- Army, Navy, Air Force, Marines --- could operate just as efficiently, and probably more so. And the taxpayers would get a big break.

***

More States Should Try Unicameral Legislature

More than ever before, states coast to coast are in deep financial trouble over bloated budgets and heavy debt. I have already suggested that one way to climb out of the red is for states to privatize most of their functions and return them to the private sector, leaving the state to act as a public watchdog and referee. No important services would be lost; they would simply be better managed.

At the same time, other states could begin economizing by following the example of Nebraska, the only state to adopt a unicameral legislature. The system is working well there and is saving Nebraskans a lot of money.

***

Let's Face It: The U.N. Has Been a Failure

Soon after the Second World War, nations of all sizes gathered in San Francisco to create the United Nations, which they believed would bring an end to wars everywhere and finally fulfill the dream of permanent peace around the globe. More than half a century later, it is quite obvious that the U.N. has been a colossal failure and that the U.S. has wound up being despised as Enemy No. 1 by many nations, despite the trillions in aid we have provided them and our haste in going to the aid of beleaguered nations.

It's time for the U.S. to dump the U.N. and join with the Major Powers to put down wars and civil strife wherever they occur to keep the peace. The U.S. and its Allies should then organize a volunteer force, formed of recruits from all nations and including ground, naval, and air units. Command of the volunteers would be rotated among the Major Powers, and the vehicles, tanks, planes, and warships required would be supplied by all the powers. Similarly, payment of the forces would be shared by each of the powers.

I submit that this will be the only way the world will ever put an end to wars and secure a permanent peace.

***

American Education Sorely in Need of Repair

What's wrong with our schools? Why do we continue to show up near the bottom of the list when our students are compared with those of other leading nations?

I would suggest that one of the reasons is the lack of discipline, particularly in grade schools and high schools. But there are other reasons, too. We have lowered expectations, demanded less of our students, and relied on grading systems that let too many poor and under-achieving students "get by."

Among the changes I would suggest is the need for all school systems, public and private, to recognize the value of home schooling in education. It makes good sense to combine regular schooling with home schooling. That would assign parents a direct role in the education of their children. We have more proof than we need to indicate that home-schooled children do much better than other children in test after test.

I would also stress the importance of "hands on" teaching at all levels, from grade schools through the college years. Nothing succeeds better in a classroom than a "show me" approach to teaching.

Another improvement I recommend is an end to "homework." I can already hear the shouts of protest and anguish, but hear me out. Today's students have too many distractions when they leave the classroom --- a variety of sports, television and films, and increased socializing. They simply don't have time to "do homework."

Does that mean I favor eliminating homework? Just the opposite. "Homework" assignments *should be done at school before students leave to return home.* School time should be set aside --- as in the present "study periods" --- for the express purpose of permitting students to complete their "homework." Teachers should be assigned to the study periods to serve as monitors and to help students with their assignments. I am positive this new system would bring a marked improvement in grades and test scores.

***

What to Do About Sexual Predators

An issue that disturbed me deeply and has affected every Governor and Legislature in the nation similarly is that of the disposition of sexual predators once they have served their prison term. Up to now, it has been the practice of all states to release these sex offenders into neighbors of their choice, with state prison systems notifying those neighborhoods of the presence of a onetime predator. Of course, that decision has drawn sharp protests from the neighbors involved.

I can't blame the neighbors. In so many of these cases, authorities acknowledge that the released prisoners are still said to be capable of repeating their crimes. Too often, they do just that, and innocent women and children are the violent victims.

I have absolutely no sympathy for these sexual predators. Psychiatrists have frequently warned authorities and the public in general that the great majority of these criminals cannot be reformed and cured of their criminal behavior.

Why do we have any sympathy for these despicable miscreants? Under the circumstances, I believe that once they have been convicted of such a heinous crime, they don't deserve to be returned to normal society and quiet neighborhoods in cities and towns. I think we should create secure campuses or centers far removed from any urban center, build simple residential quarters and whatever utilities and services are required, and consign these predators to them. A fence should encircle the entire center and it should be under heavy guard 24 hours a day.

Sound too harsh? To some persons, perhaps, but these vicious offenders are deserving of permanent incarceration away from society. Anyone who doesn't agree should have to listen to the agonized grief of families that have lost a child or young woman to a sexual predator who has been released much too soon from prison.

***

In Sports: Tale of the Prince and the Pauper

If the reader is as devoted a sports fan as I am, he or she must be deeply worried about the feast-or-famine condition of amateur and professional sports today in America.

On one hand, for example, is the serious dilemma most American colleges and universities find themselves in regarding varsity and intramural sports and the athletic and health programs that should be available to all students. Even the largest colleges and universities are finding it hard to make ends meet, despite the fact that they have football teams that attract massive crowds and radio-TV income and basketball teams that do more than break even.

By the time the income from football and basketball is distributed to pay for the many other sports and intramural programs that attract few admissions or none at all, the treasury is very slim or even in deficit.

I see great irony in all this. The colleges and universities devote considerable time, money, and effort in the development of superior athletes. Then, at the peak of their skill, the athletes move into the professional ranks and the major leagues. Suddenly, the sky's the limit.

Salaries are in six or seven figures! It is no longer startling to hear about a sports figure signing a contract giving him over $100 million over a period of six or seven years!

Ambitious lawyers and agents, seeing a gold mine, are the persons fueling this gigantic escalation in major-league salaries --- and, as usual, the fan is paying the big bills. Why can't some of this money be returned to the colleges and universities that paid all the training bills in the first place and received little for it? The prince ought to give the pauper a break.

But, hold on. I have other ideas for the sorely needed restructuring of all professional sports.

First, hundreds of thousands of students are forced to take out loans to help them complete their college schooling; in most cases, they are able to pay back the loans within a few years after graduation. Why shouldn't the same general idea apply to all the students who get a free ride through college on athletic scholarships and then go into major-league sports to become millionaires overnight?

Second, why not require that each professional team form a corporation, with shares assigned to everyone involved, including owners, executives, the manager and his staff, and each player. Instead of predetermined salaries, each member would be assigned a percentage of the annual profit. When the team did well at the gate, all members would profit handsomely. And when it flopped on the field and at the gate, all members would have to take a cut in pay, so to speak. This corporate idea could apply to all professional sports.

Third --- and this one is bound to start a dispute --- I think it's time for the Electronic Age to make its appearance in all pro sports. In baseball, umpires are lambasted continually for "guessing" about a ball or strike. Did it hit the corner and was it too high or too low? It should be easy for electronic engineers to come up with a "picture" of the plate, TV-style, which would immediately record whether a pitcher's throw was in the strike zone. The foul lines could also be controlled electronically so there would be no doubt about whether a line drive was fair or foul or that it fell inside the foul pole in right or left field.

Electronic controls could also be introduced into football, basketball, tennis, hockey, and others.

P.S. Concerning the idea of highly paid pro athletes returning some of their cash to the colleges that trained them, why shouldn't it also apply to doctors and other professionals in the top 1 percent of individual income? Hmmm. Good idea.

***

You Still Can't Legislate Morals!

Nothing taints the American political scene more dangerously than the demagogues of the Right and the Left. They are dangerous because they use a little bit of truth and a whole lot of emotional tripe in an effort to win power and control.

While the demagogues of the Left get plenty of publicity and can be detected and unmasked quite easily, those of the Right are better disguised because they travel under the colors of morality, God, and country. No better example exists than the organization calling itself the Moral Majority, which presumes to provide moral guidance for the rest of us, like it or not.

The irony of it all is that the greatest damage inflicted by the Moral Majority is upon those who most would like to improve the moral fiber of this country. Why? Because these loud-singing, hand-clapping moralists make a mockery of the very things they preach. By George! They will make law-abiding, peace-loving people of us --- if they have to subjugate every one of us to do it! They would force their strict, unforgiving moral codes on all others and write their morality into laws to ensure compliance.

I believe most Americans want a moral nation, but I'm quite sure they don't want a noisy group of fire-and-brimstone zealots dictating the rules. In the political arena, those who will be hurt most are the honest Conservatives.

As I see it, the ultraliberals, socialists, and other habitués of the American Left are silently cheering the zealots on, to the embarrassment of the Conservatives. Those who espouse moderation and those who seek morality as a choice, not a dictum, should be the strongest opponents of all demagogues --- moral and otherwise.

***

<u>A Giveaway in Disguise</u>

Quite a controversy was stoked several years ago by President Reagan's decision to hold up on a projected Law of the Sea Treaty --- until he and his administration could take a closer look at its implications. His decision was wise, and I hope other Presidents will act accordingly.

Because of my position as an assistant secretary of state back in 1975, I am well acquainted with the provisions of the treaty and what it means to our nation. Believe me, that treaty sorely needs public scrutiny and a new approach. As presently written, it would give away most of our nation's rights in the open seas, including considerable jurisdiction over resources in waters near our own coasts.

As a marine biologist and a very concerned citizen, I support the rationale for a Law of the Sea Treaty. But I would like to see an international agreement that guarantees our own requirements in the future, not one that gives away the fruit of our labors and makes available without recompense all our hard won technology in ocean exploration and research. For whom do we work?

Let's take just one of the many issues at stake, for example: Mining the ocean bottom. If our nation or any other nation bordering on ocean water undertakes risky, expensive, and time-consuming undersea activity that results in the recovery of some of the manganese-rich nodules resting at sea bottom, the finder would be required to give away much of the resources or the profits to have-not nations. Now, I submit, that is a distorted and highly punitive method of foreign aid. Haven't we given away enough of ourselves already?

***

How About a Little American Aid?
Some may think this idea a bit silly, but I will offer it partly in fun --- but just a little tongue in cheek.

I've been hearing and reading a lot about the way America's popularity has plummeted in recent years, not only among the nations of the Third World but also among those countries we have long called our Allies. The image of Uncle Sam is deeply tarnished everywhere, we're told. Some characterize us as greedy or warlike and say we're interested only in using other people in the world to enrich ourselves. Others say we are not truly desirous of winning freedom for oppressed nations, because we back tyrants and despots.

Still others, most notably some of our so-called friends, fire darts our way in world markets or extract anything they can from us, while pretending friendship in statements for the world press. Since the Marshall Plan and Truman's Point Four programs were initiated a half century ago, the United States has poured trillions into foreign aid --- to the benefit of friend and foe alike. Never in history has a single nation given so much of itself to other nations of the world. And we have asked very little in return.

My thought is this: Since the world seems to have so little respect for us at this time, let us stop foreign aid altogether for the next ten years or so and see what happens. We could apply that money instead to *American Aid* --- particularly to shore up the Social Security and Medicare programs.

Maybe it's about time Congress turned its back on those who are criticizing us from abroad. There's nothing that mandates we should be financially supporting so much of the world. Let's give a hand, for a change, to those whose money it was in the first place!

Yes, it's a foolish idea, but it would be nice for a while to see a little gratitude for all the aid we send abroad.

CHAPTER 20
PROLOGUE: A NEW APPROACH

A short time before she died in 1994, Dr. Ray and I agreed that one of the most important issues the President and Congress should tackle was the need for a truly balanced, sensible national environmental policy that satisfied scientific and environmental factors and put the interests of people above that of animals, land, and sea. Her detailed view of the need for a new environmental policy is in Chapter 6. I realize this prologue repeats some of the sentiments in that chapter. But, because this prologue is written so eloquently, I decided the repetition is worth it; it expresses her beliefs and mine more strongly than anything else she had written or spoken.

***

Through its remarkable ingenuity, the human race has developed myriad devices to improve its living conditions, its comfort, and its physical welfare.

It is true that those devices have not always been used wisely and that mankind has sometimes scarred unnecessarily the Earth that gives it substance. But that is no reason for declaring those devices inhuman or for demanding a halt to all technology, science, and progress, as some modern-day Luddites insist.

It is no coincidence that our awakening to the precious nature of the world, to its fragile environment, and to its limitations coincided with our first glimpse of this Earth from space through the eyes of astronauts, sensitive television cameras, and ingenious photographic equipment.

It was through technology that we saw ourselves as we really are, alone on one living, precious globe in space, a human family dependent on the resources of one planet, limited.

I think it was largely through that extraordinary adventure into space that we really began the first crusade for a more responsible attention to how we use our knowledge, how we put our technology to work, and how we treat the Earth that is our home.

Thus, we have witnessed an environmental movement, which has grown in vigor and strength in recent years, and much good has come from it. But some severe problems have arisen, as well, because certain strident, unreasonable voices within the movement have tended to focus only on the things that are bad, have resulted in neglect, or led to damage and exploitation.

I do not quarrel with what they say, but I remind them that, on balance, much that is quite good has come from the use of our knowledge, our sciences, our engineering, our technology.

We urgently need a new environmentalism and a new age of reason that will bring together to the discussion table those opposing sides that now seem to be irreconcilable. If, as some of the strong voices proclaim, technology has helped create the problems that anger them, they must recognize similarly that the wise use of technology --- and scientific ingenuity --- is the best, and may be the only way, to bring solutions, while avoiding the disaster of bringing the nation to a halt.

There is a middle road, and it is the path lit by knowledge, common sense, patience, and calmness, not epithets and hysterical accusations that are emotional, rather than factual. I earnestly hope America will choose the path of reason and embark on that new environmentalism before irrational decisions are made.

Printed in the United States
76059LV00011B/70